HOLY RESILIENCE

FINDING THE WAY FORWARD (A CHRISTIAN DEVOTIONAL COLLABORATION)

DEVOTIONAL COLLABORATIONS   MICHAEL LACEY
MIRANDA J CHIVERS   GRACE TERRY, MSW
LEISA WILLIAMS   PAM PEGRAM   C J WESTCOT
EMILY SMITH   MIMI EMMANUEL   N C R

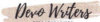

Copyright © 2021 by Michael Lacey with Story Builds Creative, Devo Writers Collaborations, and the Christian Writers' Collections.

All rights reserved. This book or any portion thereof
may not be reproduced or used in any manner whatsoever
without the express written permission of the publisher
except for the use of brief quotations in a book review. Each author owns their content and can use it at their discretion via the shared contract.
Story Builds Creative
2680 Baptist Road, Nesbit, MS 38651
Story-Builds.com
DevoWriters.com

ISBN (paperback black and white): 978-1-954838-00-0
ISBN (paperback color): 978-1-954838-01-7

Cover design, formatting, and production by Michael Lacey with Story Builds Creative.

CONTENTS

Introduction   vii

Part I
THE AUTHORS

Michael Lacey	3
Grace Terry	5
Miranda J. Chivers	7
Leisa Williams	9
Other Contributors	11

Part II
SHORT DEVOTIONALS

1. To Know Christ Through the Crisis   17
   Michael Lacey
2. Why Should I Complain for Needing You?   21
   Michael Lacey
3. Through Your Season   25
   Michael Lacey
4. I'm Rubber, You're Glue   29
   Michael Lacey
5. No More Valleys, No More Mountains   33
   Michael Lacey
6. Your True Self   37
   CJ Westcot
7. What Happens When We Break?   41
   CJ Westcot
8. Come into the Sanctuary   45
   CJ Westcot
9. Through My Silent Cries   49
   Sha-Sha Chan
10. Bouncing Back from Trauma   53
    Miranda J. Chivers

11. Obstacles are Opportunities *Pam Pegram*	57
12. We Have it All Wrong *Pam Pegram*	61
13. How to be Found Resilient *Pam Pegram*	65
14. Strength Training *Pam Pegram*	69
15. God Has a Plan for You *Pam Pegram*	73
16. Ask. Seek. Knock. *Sha-Sha Chan*	77
17. Build on Trust because Anything is Possible *Sha-Sha Chan*	81
18. Resilience through Grief *Grace Terry*	85
19. Pregnant with Promise *Emily Smith*	89
20. Up Again *NCR*	93
21. Rise Up *NCR*	97
22. Taking the First Step *Kelly Walk Hines*	101
23. Conquer the World *Kelly Walk Hines*	105
24. When it Rains, Jump in the Puddles *Kelly Walk Hines*	109

Part III
DEVOTIONAL STORIES

25. BE CAREFUL WHAT YOU ASK FOR... Mimi Emmanuel	113
26. FINDING PURPOSE IN TRAUMA Miranda J. Chivers	125
27. POUR OUT YOUR HEART Jodi Arndt	135

28. THE POWER OF GRATITUDE	143
Grace Terry	
29. CURVE BALLS	155
Leisa Williams	
30. THROW OUT YOUR CALENDARS	165
Leisa Williams	
Free Devotionals and Stories	169
Join the Next Collection	171
Last Request	173

INTRODUCTION

Holy Resilience is a collection of short daily devotions as well as longer devotional stories. To get a quick read in the morning to start your day right, jump to the Daily Devotion section. When you have more time and want to see God's faithfulness show through someone's life story, read one of the Devotional Stories in the second half of the book.

This collection is formed with various authors around the world. You may notice different spellings or styles such as "Savior" versus "Saviour". We celebrate the international feel and have retained author styles.

The viewpoints of each author do not reflect those of everyone involved. We differ on some theological issues, but our goal is to come together—despite those differences—to share messages that challenge us to be faithful through troubled times.

DISCLAIMER: if you have any issues with the theologies (which do vary slightly), or any devos in particular, please reach out to those authors directly. Each of us are passionate about the Word of God, and if we are risking blasphemy or causing damage in any way, we WANT to know. God's word is holy, and it deserves our best. Each writer is allowed to share their beliefs in a judgment-free way.

However, one core belief holds true for all of us: salvation (and thus eternity in heaven with God) is available to all who call upon the name of Jesus, as outlined in John 14:6 and John 3:16, of course.

May the real stories from these real people reflect the real God and give you tools for to have holy resilience through every season.

You are not alone. You are loved. You are here for a reason.

Godspeed,

-Michael Lacey, Story-Builds.com (and the Devo Writers Collaborations group)

As per Amazon Affiliate rules: there are affiliate links to products in this book. As an Amazon Associate, we earn from qualifying purchases.

MORE DEVO WRITERS
COLLABORATIONS

Hope When it Hurts: The Scars that Shape Us is the first book in the series, though they do not have to be read in any order. It is full of longer devotional stories—many are really like testimonies—that point to the living Hope we have in Jesus.

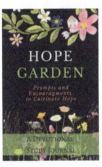

Hope Garden is a Devotional Study Journal that lays out a framework that can be approached daily or weekly, including gratitudes and a praise section with links and lyrics to worship songs. It's best in print, but the digital is a great starter.

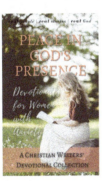

Peace in the Presence of God: A Devotional for Women with Anxiety: the third official devo writers collaboration.

SPECIAL THANKS AND REQUEST

Half of the proceeds from each Devo Writers Collaboration goes to a related charity for the first year of each book release. By purchasing this RESILIENCE devotional collection, you are supporting victims of COVID-19 and others who need our help through the Christian Relief Fund.

So, we collectively shout, "THANK YOU!" for your 'donation', and we have faith you will draw nearer to God through these heartfelt writings.

One More Request!

People need to build Resilience, cultivate Hope, and grow in Faith. The more reviews, the more readers we can attract.

To do your part, please leave an honest review on Amazon!

Thank you!

PART I
THE AUTHORS

MICHAEL LACEY

Michael is responsible for putting these collections together. With his book production company, Story Builds Creative (Story-Builds.com), he helps female Christian writers become published authors in collaborations and saving them years and thousands of dollars. If you have ever dreamt of getting your writing out there, don't hesitate to reach out to Michael at michael@michaellacey.me.

Michael writes devotions as well as fiction under the pen name M. Lacey. Get some of his stories and books at fiction.michaellacey.me.

Coming from the rich writing heritage of Mississippi, he believes in the power of words to inspire and encourage. It is a lifelong calling to put pen to paper (or fingertips to keys) for him, and he doesn't take it lightly.

His goal is to spend as much time with his family as possible, especially while his boys are young. He believes money will come and go, but time never comes back. If you'd like to support him in any way, reach out or join his mailing lists to get all of his newest content.

michaellacey.me

∽

In this book:
To Know Christ Through the Crisis
| Why Should I Complain for Needing You? | Through
Your Season | I'm Rubber, You're Glue | No More
Valleys, No More Mountains

Devotional Author Profile: https://amzn.to/3iGe5AO
Fiction Author Profile: https://amzn.to/3odupdg

GRACE TERRY

Grace Terry, MSW, writes from her lived experience as a survivor of multiple traumatic losses with the foundation of her graduate education, forty years' professional experience and advanced training in grief coaching/mentoring. She is available virtually and in person for
anything from one-to-one to conferences. Her greatest desire is to serve God by passing forward the lovingkindness God's angels have generously shown to her.

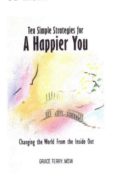

Her books, Ten Simple Strategies for a Happier You and The Spiral Pathway of Grief, are on Amazon: https://amzn.to/3iArPwS

More info at angelsabide.com

Read her devos: Resilience through Grief | The Power of Gratitude

MIRANDA J. CHIVERS

Miranda J. Chivers is a Canadian Christian writer and PTSD survivor who seeks to inspire others to overcome difficult circumstances.

She is the author of "Unequally Yoked: Staying Committed to Jesus and Your Unbelieving Spouse" which details the intimate struggles a Christian has when their spouse does not follow Christ. (ISBN 9781775189503) Her ministry includes a support group and mentoring for Christian spouses in unequally yoked marriages. She can be reached through Amazon.com/author/mirandajchivers and social media FB@mirandajchivers. Her books are available on Amazon and through Barnes & Noble via Ingram Spark Publishers.

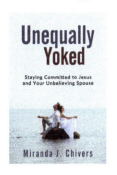

Read her devo: Finding Purpose in Trauma

LEISA WILLIAMS

Leisa was born in 1971 and brought up in Queensland. An experienced Christian school educator, she lives in Canberra with her husband, her three children, and her daughter-in-law.

She writes from her heart about her life experiences that have come from the school of hard knocks. Her views are tried and tested from many years of working  to overcome adversity in her life, as well as being founded on her Christian Biblical faith, the wise counsel and professional support from healthcare professionals, and her educational background, which includes a Master of Education degree.

leisawilliamsauthor.com

Read her devos:
Curve Balls | Throw Out Your Calendars

OTHER CONTRIBUTORS

Jodi Arndt | Pour Out Your Heart

Jodi was raised in the bootheel of Missouri, where farmland is prevalent and so is hospitality. Jodi is married to Stefan and is a mama to three spirited boys who grow her faith and her heart daily. In 2017, Jodi published her first book "Little Moments, Big God". In 2018, Jodi left the banking industry and now homeschools her boys full-time. jodiarndt.com

Sha-Sha Chan | Through My Silent Cries | Ask. Seek. Knock. | Build on Trust because Anything is Possible

Sha-Sha Chan is one of the contributing authors of the book, Beneath the Mask – Faith, Hope & Transformation in the face of Covid-19, which became #1 in Amazon's New Release in its category. facebook.com/bloggingbyfaith

Mimi Emmanuel | Be Careful What You Ask For

mimiemmanuel.com

Kelly Walk Hines | Taking the First Step | Conquering the World | When it Rains, Jump in the Puddles

My name is Kelly Walk Hines, and I reside in New Jersey. I am a 48-year-old divorced Christian mother of two wonderful adult children. I am currently dating a wonderful, kind man who has a great son. I am very happy and blessed. I have been a registered nurse since 1992. God took the trauma of my past and used it to help me relate to others and help them find healing. www.feelinghopeful.com

N.C.R. | Up Again | Rise Up

N.C.R., 20 years old, is the oldest of 8 children, and is the founder of The SunShining, host of the SunShining Podcast, and creator of SunBible. He is passionate about sharing godly resources and inspiration thoughts. He also really loves to ask questions to help people think. thesunshining.weebly.com/ncr.html

Pam Pegram | Obstacles are Opportunities | We Have it All Wrong | How to be Found Resilient | Strength Training | God Has a Plan for You

Pam Pegram is a writer, speaker and entrepreneur. She is the founder of Master What Matters, inspiring women to focus on what matters most – their relationship with Jesus. As a mentor of women in business for 20+ years, Pam loves to come alongside others to help them grow in their faith and live the abundant life.

You can find Pam's book, *Saved by Grace, Now What?*, on Amazon and her website, pampegram.com. Be sure to subscribe to her blog and follow her on social media.

Pam and her husband, Tom, live in Mississippi. They love spending time with their children and grandchildren.

∼

Emily Smith | Pregnant with Promise

Emily lives in Mississippi with her husband, Jason, and two sons Cade and Noah. She hosts the blog Song of a Sparrow. Emily is a writer, blogger, speaker, and Bible study leader. Answering the call to "Who will go?" led her to help people Jesus can use all things for His glory. songofasparrow.org

∼

CJ Westcot | Your True Self | What Happens When We Break | Come into the Sanctuary

CJ Westcot is a teacher and upcoming Christian Writer from North Mississippi. In 2019, while serving with a team in Los Angeles, God called her into ministry. Her heart for people who are hurting, and their stories of redemption are what drives her writing. CJ is passionate about walking alongside others in their journey and currently serves with the Desoto County

Dream Center, writing devotionals and recording the life-changing stories of those in the community. Her desire is that people will feel encouraged by these stories and maybe find the strength one day to tell their own.

desotodreamcenter.org

PART II
SHORT DEVOTIONALS

To Know Christ Through the Crisis

-Michael Lacey

TO KNOW CHRIST THROUGH THE CRISIS

MICHAEL LACEY

"and if children, also heirs—heirs of God and coheirs with Christ—if indeed we suffer with Him so that we may also be glorified with Him."
— Romans 8:17

Have you ever felt like you've been drug through the mud, put to shame, rejected, maybe even despised and disrespected? I have, on a few occasions, even at church. However, I knew I was pursuing God, reading His word, applying His principles, and walking in the footsteps of Christ. Rather than questioning that person's motives and their heart, I chose to let God teach me. Rather that fighting for myself, I put myself fully into God's hands, knowing that the worst thing I could think of could still be used for His glory and the advancement of His kingdom.

It is possible for your situation to make a difference in someone's life, or perhaps even in an entire organization's structure and methods. You may be a guinea pig for a failed experiment that grows the company or the people around you. If that is the case, you may never know it, but it could be worth it. For me, if God uses my pain and shame to change someone's heart, I will remain willing. However, that is in God's hands, not our own. Our job is obedience.

If you are in one of those situations or seasons—one where you know you are living righteously—don't make a big decision in the middle of the storm. Under stress, we become people we aren't normally, and so do those around us. The view is skewed by dark clouds, rain, and an ocean of distance. But when the storm clears, you'll see where you really are. Then, you can make a wise decision based on the true facts rather than the occasional storm that's sure to come in any position.

Finally, though most potently, consider Christ. Again, I ask, "Have you felt like you've been drug through the mud, put to shame, rejected, maybe even despised and disrespected? Were you walking with Jesus?" Perhaps all of this was allowed for the simple, yet profound, purpose of knowing more about Jesus in His sufferings. Perhaps you got a moment in the footsteps of Jesus? What it would mean to us to truly know what He went through... And anything that gives me more insight into Jesus is worth it all.

"We are afflicted in every way but not crushed; we are perplexed but not in despair; we are persecuted but not abandoned; we are struck down but not destroyed. We always carry the death of Jesus in our body, so that the life of Jesus may also be displayed in our body."

— 2 Cor. 4:8-10

God, I trust You. I don't always trust those around me or over me, but I trust You. Like Your Son, use me in the ways that will bring You glory and advance Your kingdom, regardless of what I think is happening. I know Your ways are bigger than ours.

Why Should I Complain for Needing You More?

-Michael Lacey

WHY SHOULD I COMPLAIN FOR NEEDING YOU?

MICHAEL LACEY

"Walking through this season is SO hard. I can't see past my face! Nearly every decision is clouded. I don't know what to choose. What do I do? Walking in this darkness makes me hungry for the light. I desperately search for any spark, any illumination."

— Me, a few times over the last year or so.

What did I do? What DO I do? I focus on the things that are constant. Seasons change, so they don't get as much of my attention anymore. I recognize that my need for God is not limited to hardship. It is constant.

. . .

Here are some constants:

- God wants us to praise Him with thanksgiving. (Ps. 69:30, 100:4; Phil. 4:6-7)
- I need Him at all times. (John 15:5, Heb. 13:6)
- He wants me to want Him, at all times, and more than I want anything else. (Ps. 121:1-8, Ex. 34:14)
- He has greater plans for me than I can imagine. (Jer. 29:11, Eph. 3:20)
- He loves me. (John 3:16, Romans 5:8)
- God is good. (1 Chr. 16:34, Ps. 25:8, Ps. 145:9)

Before all this, I used to be full of indescribable peace, but it had been replaced with uncertainty over the last 2-3 years. I find myself complaining, having to rely on God daily, sometimes hourly. And I asked myself, "Why would I complain for having to spend more time with God, for needing more of His presence?" Are those not the times that we should treasure, times when we can barely take the next breath without asking Him for it, and praising Him for the previous one?

In those times, I was so stressed and anxious that I found myself praying every hour. And in my arrogance, I complained that I 'had' to do that. "God, why must I need You every hour of every day?"

What a terrible place I was in to see it that way. Now, I thank God for that, I thank Him that my circumstances push me into His arms; that He is always there; that I am building a habit of communing with

Him constantly, regardless of what it took to get me here.

Have you felt like this, so far down in the valley you couldn't yell loudly enough for anyone to hear you? God hears us and meets us where we are. It's not so hard to worship Him on the mountaintops. What I want Him to hear are His praises being sung from the depths.

Now, when the next crazy season of life comes, I know what we need to do. Instead of complaining about the hard things, let's be thankful for them, not only the hard things but for everything large and small. Let's fix our eyes on the constants, the truths of who God is and how He loves us. Let us look to the Lord and see His great and wondrous works.

> Lord, may Your Word be my constant. I will look You first and constantly. I will work to release the weights of finances and uncertainties while trusting that You are bigger than my limited scope. If this is where I am, then this is where You want me. I will not complain that I see my need for Him, no, I will praise Him for the chance to grow closer to Him.

Through Your Season

-Michael Lacey

THROUGH YOUR SEASON

MICHAEL LACEY

"The redemptive effect of suffering lies chiefly in its tendency to reduce the rebel will."
— CS Lewis from *The Problem of Pain*

I love this quote: "The test that you're facing wasn't meant to kill you — it was designed to double you." God allows catastrophes not to divide or break us down but to multiply and make us stronger.

Do the hard thing until it's the easy thing. Dwayne "The Rock" Johnson has been called the hardest working man in any room. That inspires me when I'm nearing the end of a task, such as a jog. I study two paths: one will end my run sooner, the other will be longer and harder. Sometimes, it's that 'quick' look into the pantry and the temptation to grab a Dove chocolate instead of some unsalted almonds. I don't always choose to do the hard thing, but when I do, I don't regret it.

The difference between living like The Rock (the actor) versus the Rock (Christ) is that it is Christ who is glorified when I do the hard thing. That drives me more than any catchy sport slogan.

Here's another encouraging thought when you face temptations. It's a concept Levi Lusko explores in his book, *I Declare War*. When the enemy gets involved, he's showing his hand. He's showing that he's afraid of what you might do. He'll speak death when he knows what the power of life will do.

With all that in mind, there are times to be still, to pray and wait, to expect rather than trying to do it on your own. We know from the gospels that birds don't toil but are cared and provided for.

"Men will never become great in theology until they become great in suffering." -Spurgeon

We won't always know why something is happening or what exactly we should do. Rick Warren says, "Understanding can wait, obedience can't." It is often obedience which unlocks understanding. Steven Furtick says, "Stop living through your season and live IN it." Don't treat it like it's a steppingstone (though it may very well be) but know that God has something for you IN this season. It probably won't look anything like what you think it will.

∽

Lord, help me to not come to You for what I can get out of You but for what You can get out of me. I am open to what You are doing. Help me to take advantage of THIS moment. Help me to do the hard thing when I know it's the right thing. Then, help me to glorify You for whatever comes from it.

I'm Rubber

You're Glue

-Michael Lacey

I'M RUBBER, YOU'RE GLUE

MICHAEL LACEY

"I'm rubber, and you're glue. Whatever you say bounces off me and sticks to you."
— Childhood tease

---

*E*rase the other person in this scenario (see what I did there? I inserted another school supply item. Pretty sharp. Okay, I'm done, for real.)

Are you rubber, or are you glue? For the longest time—and still on occasion—I was glue. I allowed every difficult happening to stick to me and weigh me down. Every time another thing would go wrong, I would say, "Of course it would be me," or "That figures."

It's a common human experience, key word: common. But I'm learning that I don't want to be common. I want to have more problems, more hardships, more challenges... more opportunities to rise above.

"You're crazy!" You may be shouting.

Yes, something isn't normal in my head, and I don't want it to be. Maybe the Bible can say it better than me... who am I kidding? Of course, it can!

"Concerning this, I pleaded with the Lord three times that it would leave me. But he said to me, "My grace is sufficient for you, for my power is perfected in weakness." Therefore, I will most gladly boast all the more about my weaknesses, so that Christ's power may reside in me. So, I take pleasure in weaknesses, insults, hardships, persecutions, and in difficulties, for the sake of Christ. For when I am weak, then I am strong."
-2 Corinthians 12:8-10 CSB

You see, after years—decades, really—of struggles and hardships (many like those you have faced), God has brought me to a new place. He has changed my molecular structure; I am no longer glue, I am rubber. New challenges bounce off of me. The enemy throws things that don't stick... well, sometimes they do, but not as much as before.

I will add a caveat to this illustration. As a friend pointed out to me, we don't want to be so resistant that we become hardened. That's the thing about rubber. Usually, it's still soft and must be in order to stay effective. If it rots or dries out though, it's useless. I will stay vigilant that I don't become hardened and unusable.

Let's be rubber and not glue. As best we can, we'll let hardships bounce off while we watch our Savior. Isaiah 40:31 has multiple translations; some say those who trust in the Lord while others say hope or wait. Sometimes we are just waiting as He renews our strength, and sometimes we are watching Him work and worshiping Him for it.

And as we fix our eyes on the Lord, we will:

- imitate Him (Eph. 5:1)
- reflect Him (2 Cor. 3:18)
- be more like Him (1 Cor. 11:1)
- be light to the darkness around us (Eph. 5:8)
- purify ourselves by our obedience to the truth, show sincere brotherly love, love constantly from pure hearts (1 Peter 1: 22)
- get life as we give it (Phil. 1:21)
- live out hope while worshiping the living Hope (1 Pet. 1:2)

God, help me to stay so focused on You that attacks and distractions bounce off. And when I let things stick to me, please give me the mind to let you pull them away. Change my structure to be one that glorifies You rather than discrediting myself. I am a child of God. You are my refuge.

No More Valleys No More Mountains

-Michael Lacey

NO MORE VALLEYS, NO MORE MOUNTAINS

MICHAEL LACEY

"Anyone who finds his life will lose it, and anyone who loses his life because of me will find it."
— Matthew 10:39 CSB

---

*L*ose everything because of a pursuit of God, an existential crisis to the core that strips these things that I've used to define my "life"—when our buildings crumble, the view opens up. And out of the rubble, we begin to build on a true foundation.

I sometimes equated my life to Job's, but I knew that was just ridiculous. However, I saw failure after failure, and loss after loss, all while I believe I was being righteous, or at least striving to be.

Now I know that God allowed those tough times so

that He and I can walk closer, so that the world's calls would sound a bit quieter each day, so I would focus not on mountaintops or valleys but rather on Him, and let my location and circumstance have no bearing on my worship.

Like Job's story, God allows catastrophes not to divide or break us down but to multiply, to make us stronger: stronger in Him, His word, His truth, and in faith.

Still struggling—sometimes that's where you will live—the testimony isn't always "how God brought me through," sometimes it's just the fact that I'm staying faithful—imagine Job in the middle. He couldn't convince people to do as he was doing, even his wife said to curse God. That's where I feel I am—and if that's where I'll stay, then it's okay. I don't want to see mountains and valleys. I want to see God. If people can see Him and His fruit in me, regardless of how "successful and blessed" I seem, then I am going the right way.

If I can truly trust the faithfulness of God, then it doesn't matter what happens to me or us. I know that He will bring us through. ***God will show you through and grow you through.***

~

God, now I know that You allow hard times so that You and I can walk closer, so that the world's calls would sound a bit quieter each day, so I would focus not on mountaintops or valleys but rather on You and let my location and circumstance have no bearing on my worship.

Your True Self

-CJ Wescot

YOUR TRUE SELF

CJ WESTCOT

But Moses protested to God, "Who am I to appear before Pharaoh? Who am I to lead the people of Israel out of Egypt?" God answered, "I will be with you."
— Exodus 3:11-12a

"I can't do this."

How many times have you spoken that phrase into existence over your life? At one time or another we have all felt the weight of our shortcomings. The things we feel disqualify us. From love. From serving. From ministry. But what if our weakness is the key to fulfilling our divine calling? To pushing on.

God has a pretty stellar record of calling broken and damaged people to do BIG things. So, what makes you think that He couldn't do the same with you? God's desire is to use you despite your broken and messy parts. So why are you fighting it?

If we are ever going to find our true selves, then we must start focusing on our view of who we ARE in Christ instead of fixating on who we WERE without HIM.

Take Moses, for example. Here's a man who ran as far from his past as he could and remade himself. We're talking wilderness shepherd mountain man. Yet God came to Moses in that wilderness as a burning bush, calling him by name to help free his people and lead them into the Promised Land. What an honor, right? God could have called anyone, but he chose Moses. And wouldn't you know it, the first thing out of his mouth wasn't, "YES, let's storm that city and do this thing!" but rather, *"Who am I?"*

Isn't it funny that you and I are asking God the exact same question?

"WHO AM I?"

Why are we so quick to question God? Better yet, why do we forget who God has called us to be? Take comfort in knowing that Moses needed that same reminder. He was holding onto the guilt and shame of his past and what he needed was to be reminded that God loved him and would meet him exactly where he was in that moment.

It's that simple.

You are a child of God, called by name to a greater purpose. And God wants to reveal that purpose, if we would only allow Him to move despite our weakness. If God can use Moses and his brokenness, then God can certainly redeem and redefine our messy lives. All we have to do is embrace who HE is calling us to be; broken pieces and all.

So, WHY was Moses so quick to question God? Was he worried that God would abandon him or what others might think? I believe the answer is that he was afraid to be THE REAL MOSES. Once he stopped fighting his thoughts and trusted that God would be there every step of the way, he stepped confidently into his identity in Christ.

Neil T. Anderson wrote, *"The more you reaffirm who you are in Christ, the more your behavior will begin to reflect your true identity."*

The question now is, when will you stop fighting the contradiction that you aren't good enough for what God is calling you to do? It's time to step out on faith and be the real you. Your TRUE SELF.

Father, teach me to be still. Help me to see myself for who I am in your eyes. I know now that I can't continue to carry my past. So, I will trust in who YOU are and step into who You created me to be. Amen.

What Happens when *You Break?*

-CJ Wescot

WHAT HAPPENS WHEN WE BREAK?

CJ WESTCOT

This is what the Sovereign LORD says: "Look! I am going to put breath into you and make you live again! I will put flesh and muscles on you and cover you with skin. I will put breath into you, and you will come to life. Then you will know that I am the LORD."
— Ezekiel 37:5-6 NLT

Have you ever stretched a rubber band to the point of breaking? There is something hypnotic in the continuous extension and bouncing back, never knowing when it might snap. Sometimes circumstances in our lives leave us feeling like a rubber band being pulled and stressed beyond our limits. But what happens when we break?

Several years ago, I found myself struggling to keep my mental health and marriage together. My anger and past had finally caught up with me and the safe world that I had wrapped myself in suddenly began collapsing in around me. My husband left and my mental health was hanging on by a thread. I wish I could say that I chose to lean into the Lord for guidance, but instead I turned to the world and began searching for my own answers. I chose to put on the "brave face" and pretended I had it together. But the stress and strain of it all caused me to spiral until one day it took its toll. The rubber band had snapped. I broke.

Paralyzed with grief and fear, I became this shell of a person who walked around lifeless and empty. Desperate for answers. I can remember one night lying in bed angry, literally screaming at God. I questioned His goodness and even His existence in my life. "God, where are You? What lesson could you possibly be teaching me through this pain?" In most narratives this would be the moment where I detail perfect surrender. But that's not my story. If I am being honest, it took several years for me to understand why God had allowed me to stay in that season of life. You see, looking back, it was in those dark and desperate moments that I began to slowly understand surrender. Sure, I still wanted to control and fix the situation on my own, but the more tired I became, the more I was willing to lay it all at the feet of Jesus. And there He was, waiting for me in my own valley of dry bones.

The lesson that God has for us is not always what we want to hear. There are times when He needs us to break. For it's in the broken and empty places of our lives that God wants to meet us and breathe life. Only HE can make us whole, but we must be willing to surrender. Over the years I have come to understand what God was teaching me and continues to teach me through the harder seasons. Like in Ezekiel 37, we may find ourselves in a valley of dry bones, spiritually dead and hopeless like the people of Israel. But the true test comes when we choose to surrender it all and trust that God is capable of not only reviving us but giving us NEW life.

Father God, walk with me in this valley where I find myself broken and hopeless. Help me trust that You are the one who brings life. I will rest in the knowledge that You will never abandon or forsake me but will be there waiting to breathe new life back into these dry bones. Amen.

Come into the
Sanctuary

-CJ Wescot

COME INTO THE SANCTUARY

CJ WESTCOT

So, Hannah ate and then she pulled herself together, slipped away quietly, and entered the sanctuary. The priest Eli was on duty at the entrance to God's Temple in the customary seat. Crushed in soul, Hannah prayed to God and cried and cried—inconsolably.

— 1 Samuel 1:9-10 MSG

Have you ever carried the pain of a secret or a deep hurt in your life? Something that you felt separated you from others. Maybe you retreated or tucked the pain away for fear of abandonment and ridicule. But truly, what you've really lost is trust.

I have a friend who experienced a deep betrayal

early in her marriage. They did what most young couples would do and turned to their church family for guidance. Sadly, they were turned away with no help, which left a scar on their hearts, but they still had a longing for reconciliation. My friend knew that God was for them and when others would have chosen to walk away, they chose God. With determination and faith, they decided that restoration was only possible if they made Jesus the center of their hopes, their hearts, and their trust in one another. It was a long road and at times lonely, but what God taught them through this is that their hearts were not made to depend upon this world for answers but uniquely designed to find fulfillment in the ONE who is constant.

I love the story of Hannah in 1 Samuel because she isn't ashamed to carry her anguish to God's sanctuary. Quietly she suffered, feeling forgotten and punished for her inability to bear a child. Ridiculed and ignored by those closest to her, she lost all hope. Hannah could have allowed her pain to consume her, but with a broken spirit she chose to walk into the sanctuary, cry out on bended knee before God, and ask for restoration of her heart and faith. Hannah's willingness to cry out to God despite her suffering is a great example of how we can bring our brokenness to the Lord, but we must choose to lean into HIM.

Maybe your story is like my friends. A past hurt that has left scars on your heart, or maybe your wound is still fresh. No matter your story, you can always find peace in knowing that you have a Heavenly Father who is there to restore hope to the hopeless and boundless joy to the broken. His answer may not always look like what you were expecting, but you will never know until you choose to walk into HIS sanctuary.

Father God, help me to turn to You and not this world for answers. I carry brokenness and hurt and long to feel you close to my heart. Help me to remember that Hannah's cries to You did not go unheard. Hear my heart cries, Lord, and renew my spirit. Let me feel Your loving arms around me as I come into your sanctuary and kneel before You. Father, thank You for Your love. You satisfy and fulfill every part of my broken heart because You are the bread of life. Amen.

Through My Silent Cries

-Sha-Sha Chan

THROUGH MY SILENT CRIES

SHA-SHA CHAN

"Why are you downcast, O my soul? Why so disturbed within me? Put your hope in God, for I will yet praise Him, my Savior and my God."
— Psalm 43:5

Reading about the believers who were earnestly praying for Peter and how God sent an angel to rescue him in prison (Acts 12), I am reminded of how much the LORD has answered my prayers in many different ways.

Even as faithful followers of Christ, we are not exempt from trials, hardships, and troubles. Sometimes, it's even piled up in a heap, one trouble after the other.

There are days when I just ask God to get me out of

the situation and there are days when I just pray for the grace and the strength to overcome.

But there are also times when I do not intentionally pray about something. I just silently cry when I lie down in bed. My inner longings in my thoughts. Not actually, verbally, and consciously lifting it up to God—just silent longings that I don't even dare to blurt out because I know it's not possible.

These silent cries, the ones I do not want anyone to see and do not even speak about, not even to God (at least from my point of view), are the ones He chooses to answer with a grand Cinderella entrance!

Every time this happens, I'm just in awe when He does that! And now I make a loud and ugly cry because I'm mind-blown and beyond grateful that He really sees me and knows me!

It is during these moments that I'm assured of His presence in my life. It confirms to me that He is real, that He truly loves me and cares about me.

Because of this, I can always move forward and put my hope and trust in Him. That there will be better days ahead. He is indeed the God of the impossible.

Father, I worship you! You are truly worthy of all praise. I'm just in awe of You. Thank You for loving me the way You do and for always assuring me of Your presence and Your power. That nothing is impossible with You. Forgive me for my unbelief. And for the times I do not lift up to

You the things that I should be praying about, knowing that it is only You who will be able answer and respond to it. In Jesus' name, Amen!

Bouncing Back from Trauma

-Miranda J. Chivers

BOUNCING BACK FROM TRAUMA

MIRANDA J. CHIVERS

"We are hard-pressed on every side, but not crushed; perplexed, but not in despair; persecuted, but not abandoned; struck down, but not destroyed."
— 2 Corinthians 4:8-9

Have you been "hard pressed on every side?"

This encouraging passage in 2 Corinthians 4:8-9 reminds me that God is the author of my life. If I give Him the pen to rewrite my circumstances, I can trust that my story will have a happy ending.

As a PTSD survivor, facing my fears is a daily challenge, but giving up or quitting are not options. My trials have taught me human power is frail, but God's grace gives resilience.

Resilience conveys the image of bouncing back.

Have you ever compared the springiness of a new rubber ball to an old one? As this material ages and dries, it loses the rebound effect. Eventually, it's worthless.

Trauma strips our bounce and wears us down—chipping away at our relationships, productivity, finances and mental and physical health. Like an old rubber ball, the effects of crisis make us feel used up and useless.

When self-confidence shatters, it's easy to become discouraged, struggle with decision-making, feel powerless, and worry about the future. We may question our faith and battle depression. If we stay stuck here, life doesn't improve. We can't wish away our circumstances. We must do something.

The effects of trauma are challenging, but recovery is more so. Intuitively, we know we must push to jump over the wall of pain, but "how to carry on" can stump us.

Grief is a normal experience following loss. It helps us to focus on positive memories, place events in proper perspective, and shift us into new directions. It's important to take this pause to re-evaluate our paths, goals, and relationships. This helps us embrace our vulnerabilities and gain the strength to step into recovery.

To effectively bounce back, we need to accept and forgive the past, and let go of the fear of the future. God's word is the lifeline to help us do that.

The Bible is a priceless source of wisdom and reassurance through times of trouble. God's grace and mercy shines through the trials of biblical characters such as David, Daniel, Job, and the Apostles. These stories build confidence and prove that God never leaves nor forsakes us. During dark days, they've given me the mental energy I've needed to keep going.

My struggles with complex trauma have taught me that regardless of my circumstances, God can reinvent my future. My responsibility is to shift and follow His lead. As I regain resilience and adapt to my new normal, the sting of the pain lessens.

I don't know what tomorrow brings, but my bounce comes in trusting Him who holds the future. And that is enough for me to embrace Paul's words: *"Forgetting the things that are behind and reaching out for the things that are ahead." Philippians 3:13.*

1. How's your resilience? Are you more of a fresh rubber ball or an old tired one? How can you regain your bounce?
2. Letting go of resentment helps us increase resiliency. What do you need to do to forgive the past, accept the present, and face the future?

∽

Lord, I'm feeling alone and overwhelmed and discouraged. I want to bounce back and be the light to the world that You want me to be. Please give me the strength and courage to overcome. In Jesus' name.

Our Obstacles *are* *Opportunities*

—Pam Pegram

OBSTACLES ARE OPPORTUNITIES

PAM PEGRAM

My brethren, count it all joy when you fall into various trials, knowing that the testing of your faith produces patience. But let patience have its perfect work, that you may be perfect and complete, lacking nothing.

—James 1:2-4

---

*C*ount it all joy? It seems crazy and we wonder if God really expects us to be thankful for the obstacles we face as we pursue His purpose for our life. How can we find joy in something that causes us conflicts, sufferings, and troubles? Well, let's dig a little deeper... the word "count" is a financial term that actually means evaluate. Could it be that God is telling us to change our attitude about our trials? After all, isn't our transformation all about having a new attitude and learning to see things from God's perspective?

Of course, we are not being instructed to pursue struggles or to pretend that trials are enjoyable. They are not. The trials that we encounter in our lives are often painful and difficult to navigate. What James is teaching us is that our trials have a purpose. They are put there to produce something good and to purge things which are not good. So, when we look at our trials from a higher view, we can have a positive expectation knowing that God will use it for good.

God uses our trials to test our faith and teach us patience. My granddaughters have been taught that to be patient means to wait without complaining. Do we do that? Do we wait on the Lord, without moaning, groaning, and complaining? James tells us that this patience can transcend our simple explanation of being patient and includes the idea of being steadfast under pressure, having the staying power that turns what we might perceive as an obstacle into an opportunity. Our trials present us with the opportunity to be made perfect and complete.

We should not see our hard days as God's punishment for our sins. Instead, we are to view them as opportunities to joyfully grow our faith and mature to become more like Christ. You see, there is a vast difference in acting Christlike and becoming like Him. God is not concerned with our outward appearance; He is concerned with the condition of our heart. If we never had a hard day, why would we need God, how would we learn to trust Him, and how would we discover His goodness?

We can count it all joy because God is going to use every obstacle we face to mature us and transform us.

They are a part of our Christian journey. They are opportunities that show up without warning to test our faith and to produce the quality of endurance. They teach us resilience. This is who we are to be, what we are to do. In spite of our suffering, we know that God is in control. We are upheld by His power. We place our trust in Him.

> God, you are good! We praise You in every season because we know You are using them all for good in our life. Help us to stay our course and keep our eyes fixed on You. We live to bring honor and glory to Your name!

We Have it All Wrong

-Pam Pegram

WE HAVE IT ALL WRONG

PAM PEGRAM

"But what things were gain to me, these I have counted loss for Christ. Yet indeed I also count all things loss for the excellence of the knowledge of Christ Jesus my Lord, for whom I have suffered the loss of all things; and count them as rubbish, that I may gain Christ."
— Philippians 3:7-8

If we are not careful, we can buy into the world's answer to the point of our life. We can place value on things that really have none. We can confuse pursuing our God-given purpose with living the American dream, going for our goals, and seeking our own happiness. If we do, we have it all wrong.

Paul's lineage could be traced back to Israel. He was

from the highly regarded tribe of Benjamin, which had produced the first king of Israel and had formed the foundation for the restored nation. He called himself a Hebrew of the Hebrews, a model Jew. He was highly educated and defended the letter of the Jewish law. He had accomplished much. My guess is that he was respected and admired among his peers.

You may know the rest of his story. He vigorously attacked those who believed in Jesus and even had some put to death. He had an encounter with Jesus—the resurrected Messiah—that changed everything. Can you relate? Can you look back and consider your life before Jesus and your life after Jesus and feel a connection to Paul's radical transformation?

In Philippians 3, Paul shares his story—his testimony. Take time to read and study all 21 verses of this chapter. Paul tells us that all of the things he believed to be important, became unimportant after he encountered Jesus. He acknowledges that he had it all wrong. He boldly proclaims that nothing—absolutely nothing—compares to knowing Jesus. His own righteousness—appearing to be good—was worthless because true righteousness comes through Christ. It is a matter of our faith, not of our works.

There is more. In verse 10, Paul states, "that I may know Him." This is not referring to an intellectual knowledge, but instead a relational knowledge—one that produces intimacy. We can experience intimacy with Jesus and the ongoing power of His resurrection. This does not mean that all our days will be easy. We are sure to know suffering, because He suffered for us. And just like He died, we are to die to our self every single day and place Him and His will above our own. And just like He was resurrected, so will we be. Our citizenship is in heaven—we are not of this world.

We are to "press on" as Paul says. We have been invited into more. Let's not settle for just knowing *about* Jesus. Let's not stop seeking Him because we have already accepted Him as our Savior. Let's pursue to know Him intimately and surrender our life to live for Him, because He is the prize. Let's make it our goal to "lay hold of that for which Christ Jesus has also laid hold of me." Let's pursue the upward call—the plan God has for us—relentlessly. Let's not get it all wrong. Let's remember nothing matters more than our relationship with Jesus.

God, forgive me for valuing myself and my pursuits above You and Your purpose for me. Today, I surrender all of me to all of You! I press on to do what You have for me to do and to become who You have called me to be.

How to Be Found Resilient

-Pam Pegram

HOW TO BE FOUND RESILIENT

PAM PEGRAM

"Keep your heart with all diligence,
    for out of it spring the issues of life.
Put away from you a deceitful mouth,
and put perverse lips far from you.
Let your eyes look straight ahead,
and your eyelids look right before you.
Ponder the path of your feet,
and let all your ways be established."
— Proverbs 4:23-26

Why are we surprised when we experience suffering? Jesus told us we would have tough times in this world, but in Him we can have peace. Scripture reminds us that we can be confident and courageous when we place our trust in God. So, if that is true, why do we struggle to bounce back after a tragedy, crisis, or other life-altering changes?

During hard times, we often allow doubt and despair to penetrate our heart. We let well-meaning family and friends run to our rescue instead of us running to the Rescuer. We entertain thoughts filled with fear and doubt and question how we will endure. We wallow in the mire of self-pity, disappointment, and fear of the unknown. Why do we lose sight of what we say we believe to be true?

God tells us in His word to guard our hearts above everything else. It is our inner core, making us who we are. Out of it, flows our thoughts, feelings, desires, will, and choices. We risk falling into pride, anger, and temptation. That is why we are instructed in Philippians 4:8 to take every thought captive. Meditating on the truth of God's word will help us build a protective covering over our heart.

We are to put away a deceitful mouth and perverse lips. This refers to us saying anything that twists, distorts, perverts, or misrepresents the truth. Instead, as children of God, we are to recall the promises He has given us all throughout scripture. We are to remember that He will never leave us or forsake us, that we can do all things through Him, that He loves us and is with us, therefore we are never alone.

We let our eyes look straight ahead—keeping our focus on God and His goodness. We lock eyes with Him—just like Peter did when he stepped out to walk on the water with Jesus. We don't look back and we don't look down—we look forward and we run to Him.

We place our faith in Him and trust Him with our tomorrow.

We ponder the path of our feet and we wait on the Lord. We remember that God has a plan for us—not to harm us, but to give us hope and a future. We boldly take each step forward as He reveals them one at a time. No need to run out in front of Him; no need to linger behind. We walk with Him.

God is asking us to have a heart devoted to Him and His purposes, truthfulness in our speech, a steadiness of our gaze and a resilience in pursuing His goal for our life—regardless of our circumstances. We cannot do it on our own. But when we place our trust in Him, He is surely enough to help us, to comfort us, and to use all things for good in our life. God is enough.

God, help me! Help me to guard my heart and fix my gaze on You. You are my Rescuer, the only One I truly need. As I encounter difficult times in my life, help me to be strong and courageous as I place my trust in You.

Strength Training

-Pam Pegram

STRENGTH TRAINING

PAM PEGRAM

"But those who wait on the Lord shall renew their strength; they shall mount up with wings like eagles, they shall run and not be weary, they shall walk and not faint."
— Isaiah 40:31

The past 12 months have been challenging, to say the least. I have lost a grandson, my sweet Daddy, and the company I have worked with for 23 years has closed its doors. My heart has been broken, my dreams have shattered, and my plans rattled. Loss is hard, grief comes in waves, and the unknown is scary. During difficult times we have a choice—fall deep into despair or rest on the promises of God.

Had I experienced this year when I was younger, my

response might have been different. I might have become bitter, lashed out at God, and took matters into my own hands. But I know better. I have experienced the goodness of the Lord; I have found His promises to be true, and I have learned that I can trust Him even when I do not understand or have all of the answers.

Those on the outside look at my life and my family and think it has been easy. Those in my inner circle know our reality. We have been through a lot. While the challenges have been great, the faithfulness of God has been greater. He has been there every step of the way—and this year has been no different. When I cried out and shook my fist in God's face after the loss of my grandson, He lovingly whispered to me that Woods was right there with Him. Woods was already experiencing everything I would have hoped for him. As the first Christmas without Daddy drew near, God reminded me that he was a part of a celebration I could not even imagine. No doubt, my dad was having his best Christmas ever! And as my career came to a close and my future uncertain, there was peace—peace because I knew that God had a plan, and it was good.

The promise above has become my life verse. God gave it to me during a difficult time and He brings me back here over and over and over again. To wait on the Lord is to have confident expectation, to place our hope in Him and to truly believe that He will do what He has promised. This is what it means to have faith in God. Every time we flex that faith muscle, *"He gives His power to the weak and to those who have no might He increases strength"* (verse 29).

Nothing can compare to the power of God. When

we tap into His power, we can keep going no matter what we may endure. God is never surprised or caught off guard. He uses our hard days to draw us closer to Him. As we come to know Him in a more intimate way, we recognize that we are not here for ourselves—but here to step into the plan He has for us and to live a life that glorifies our One True God.

God, I place my hope in You and in You alone. I trust you and your plan for me. Thank You for strengthening me and empowering me to do all you ask of me. I will live the rest of my days bringing honor and glory to Your name.

God has a Plan *For You*

-Pam Pegram

GOD HAS A PLAN FOR YOU

PAM PEGRAM

"Though a righteous person falls seven times, he will get up,
   but the wicked will stumble into ruin."
   — Proverb 24:16

Throughout God's word we read admonitions to overcome hardships (Romans 12:21), to press on (Philippians 3:13-15), and to persevere in midst of trials (James 1:12). We are given many examples of people who suffered, struggled, and faltered, but continued on to follow God's plan for their life. Moses, Abraham, and Paul—just to name a few. Resilience seems to be the norm for these heroes of faith. Is it to be the norm for us?

As we read scripture, it seems like an easy choice for

these spiritual giants. Abraham was called to leave his country and his people to travel to an undesignated land. Like us, Abraham and his family failed God over and over again. Yet, God had a plan to use Abraham. Moses was meek and stuttered. Like us, he argued with God, assuring Him that someone else would be a better choice. Yet, God had a plan to use Moses. Despite their shortcomings, each time God called their name, they would simply respond, "Here I am." It was not that God couldn't find them and they were letting Him know where they were. It was their way of acknowledging that they were available to God and ready to do whatever He asked of them.

Paul? Well, his is a bit different story. He was on his way to Damascus to persecute Christians when he had an encounter with Jesus. He was blinded by "the Light," which demonstrated his spiritual blindness. Once he was healed, so were his evil ways, and he was filled with the Holy Spirit. He received his sight, arose, and was baptized. Like us, Paul had a past that he thought would disqualify him from being of use to the Lord. Yet, God had a plan to use Paul. He would spend the rest of his life—even after being beaten, stoned, thrown in jail, and more—proclaiming the good news of Jesus.

These 3 men were resilient in their pursuit of God and His plan for their life. Like us, they were not perfect, eloquent, or pure. In fact, they were full of questions, doubts, and fears. They had a choice—a choice that would reveal what they truly believed. They could focus on their failures and hardships or they could look up and trust the One who called their name. What will you do? You see, in spite of you and your past, God has a plan for you. Will you continue to argue with God and question His plan? Or will you look up, get up, and boldly step into the plan He has specifically for you? Will you say, "Here I am!"

> God, here I am! Although I am unsure of how You can use me, I will say, 'Yes' to You. I will trust You and step boldly into the plan and purpose You have for me. I will be resilient and seek You no matter what comes my way.

Ask. Seek. Knock.

-Sha-Sha Chan

ASK. SEEK. KNOCK.

SHA-SHA CHAN

"Ask, and it will be given to you; seek, and you will find; knock, and it will be opened to you. For everyone who asks receives, and the one who seeks finds, and to the one who knocks it will be opened."

— Matthew 7:7-8, ESV

One October morning, I was reading about the account of Peter's denial when he was lurking outside the courtyard where Jesus was being questioned.

When I came to the part where he remembers what Jesus told him earlier during the Passover meal, (Matthew 26:34) that he would deny him three times before the rooster crowed that morning...

...I just had one question for Jesus.

"Lord, how did you feel when Peter, your friend, denied you?"

I closed my eyes for a second and suddenly, I saw Jesus' eyes! Just His eyes. Through His eyes, I saw His answer and it was LOVE. Kneeling down with my face touching the floor, I just cried and cried.

My limbs felt weak. My whole body was trembling. I couldn't believe Jesus was actually answering my question!

You see, I was raised in a Christian family. Being a Sunday school kid, I knew all the Bible stories and I was actively participating in our church activities ever since I could remember.

Surrounded by God's people, I heard about Him in sermons and in Bible studies. I read about Him in the Bible or in Christian literature, but never had I encountered Jesus this way.

Never had I felt so loved by Him. Since then, my walk with Him has never been the same. That one encounter changed my life forever.

I felt empowered. I knew that because He was real in my life, I could overcome anything.

Whenever I read the Bible, the words just come to life and jump right out of the book. I feel excited and thankful, it's just unbelievable.

Prior to this, I was asking God, "How come I don't hear Him?"

I felt sort of envious when my boss who was doing Bible studies with us always said, "God told me this..." "God said this to me..."

So, for many months, I actually kept on asking God, "Why don't I hear You?"

"Why can't I have that kind of relationship that she has with you?"

"Haven't I known You for almost my entire life?"

"I have been faithfully reading Your word and praying and attending church, but why can't I hear You?"

Imagine my shock when this happened, and Jesus finally decides to show up.

This is one life-changing experience that no one can really take away. Every time I go back to this moment in my life, I just can't help but thank the Lord for showing up like that.

So, to you, friend, if you have been asking God your questions, if you have been earnestly seeking Him for the longest time, if you have been knocking at His door to the point where your knuckles are about to bleed, don't give up.

He sees you. He hears. And He knows your deepest desires.

In His perfect time, you are going to get your answers. You are going to find Him, and He is going to open that door for you.

> Father, thank you because You are real. You know me better than I know myself. Give me the desire to seek You and know You more each day. And as I know You, I pray that You would encounter me in a special way that only You could do. In Jesus' name, Amen!

Build on Trust because *Anything is Possible*

-Sha-Sha Chan

BUILD ON TRUST BECAUSE ANYTHING IS POSSIBLE

SHA-SHA CHAN

"And Elisha prayed, "Open his eyes, LORD, so that he may see." Then the LORD opened the servant's eyes, and he looked and saw the hills full of horses and chariots of fire all around Elisha." — 2 Kings 6:17

---

*D*o I find it easy or hard to believe that God can do a miracle in my life?

I was pondering on this question and I couldn't give a clear-cut one-word answer if it's easy or hard.

After all, it is not a question that can be satisfied with a yes or no answer alone.

It is hard.

More so at the beginning, because I can't see the end.

I feel like I'm in a dark tunnel. The journey ahead is long and all I can see is what is right in front of me. So,

I find myself constantly needing God's own encouragement to keep me going. To keep on hearing His voice to remind me that He is with me.

Maybe it is also because I have my own expectations of how God is going to answer my prayers. I want the answers under my own terms. That instant experience that says, "I want it now!"

And because this is my expectation, I get disappointed more often than not.

I need to remind myself that His thoughts and His ways are higher than mine. He knows what is up ahead and He holds my future. That I could never be on the same level if I insist on doing things my way.

My heart and mind, then, have to be aligned and attuned to His. Because if we're not on the same page, we will never meet, and I will never understand.

Alignment. Wouldn't it be easier if we were looking at the same page, at the same thing?

Just like when Elisha asked God to open the eyes of his servant so that he could see who was behind them and not be afraid.

Attunement. Would you find it easier to trust if you knew exactly who you were talking to?

The more you know about God's attributes and His character, the more trust builds up in you.

When buying something, for example, don't you read up and research the product thoroughly and check on the reviews or the testimonials of people who have used it?

Knowing builds trust.

Meditate on God's word and who He is.

How powerful and mighty. How He is above and

beyond natural law. How He has full control and authority over all creation.

This tells me that if He is able to bring the dead to life, make the barren woman with child, part the Red Sea, and have chariots of fire as armies, then anything is possible!

Miracles in my life and in yours are possible.

> Father, You are an awesome God! There is nothing too difficult for You. Help me see You for who You are and what You can do. Open my eyes just like how you opened the eyes of the servant so that he could see. Bring to remembrance everything that You have done for me in the past so that I can continue to hold on to You in difficult times. Give me the desire to seek You every day and meditate on Your power and might. In Jesus' name, Amen!

Resilience through Grief

-Grace Terry

RESILIENCE THROUGH GRIEF

GRACE TERRY

"What a wonderful God we have—He is the Father of our Lord Jesus Christ, the source of every mercy, and the one who so wonderfully comforts and strengthens us in our hardships and trials. And why does He do this? So that when others are troubled, needing our sympathy and encouragement, we can pass on to them the same help and comfort God has given us."

—2 Corinthians 1:3-4 (Living Bible)

In 1984, I experienced three traumatic losses. The first was sudden, unexpected termination of employment. I was just a few years out of graduate school and working diligently to establish myself as a mental health professional at a time and in a community which was not supportive of female professionals. Being downsized was emotionally and financially devastating.

Before I found a new position there was a sudden, unexpected divorce and relocation. I was stunned, angry, terrified, and shattered. A Christian since childhood, I could not understand how this had happened. I entered the only agnostic period of my life, doubting the existence of anything or any One in the universe that made any kind of sense at all.

The third traumatic loss that year was the sudden death of my beautiful, vibrant, fifty-six-year-old mother in an automobile accident. In spite of my anger, fear, and doubts, God sent angels – friends, family, and strangers who extended themselves to show lovingkindness to me and to my family.

The emotional and spiritual support was absolutely palpable. The kindness of strangers touched me most deeply and renewed my faith in a loving God.

Since then, there have been additional losses – my father's sudden death two years after my mother's, a second divorce a year after that, traumatizing betrayals, forced estrangement, financial reverses, and others. Miraculously, many comforters appeared over the years to guide me on the spiral pathway of grief.

I believe my grief companions appeared because I desperately sought their guidance and was willing to accept it. I am infinitely grateful to all who loved me through life's most challenging twists, turns, and transitions. Without the ongoing kindness and wisdom of countless angels (messengers from God) along the pathway, I could not have survived.

Some were flesh and blood human angels. Some were furry and four-legged. Some were musicians, poets, artists, or authors – both living and immortal. And yes, looking back I believe some were celestial. All helped to make me the person I am today – relatively sane, reasonably functional, still learning as I plod the spiral pathway of grief, peaceful most of the time, and daily thankful.

I have since become a professional grief educator and grief coach. I recently wrote and published a book about my experiences, titled *"The Spiral Pathway of Grief: The Traveler's Guidebook."* My life's purpose is to pass forward the lovingkindness that has been generously extended to me.

I believe this is God's plan for us. We receive care and comfort when we need it, then pass it forward to others. *Passing love forward is not an obligation. It is a privilege.*

> Prayer for today: Dear God, thank You for loving me even when I am pathetically unlovely. Please work in and through me to bring Your love and encouragement to those I meet today. I give you all the glory. Amen.

Pregnant with Promise

-Emily Smith

PREGNANT WITH PROMISE

EMILY SMITH

Resilience: the ability to bounce back.

Have you ever had a season that seems like everything is going wrong and there's no relief in sight? Unfortunately, that is what life is about: Taking the hits and bouncing back. Friend, I have been there. There was a period of about 4 years that my husband and I didn't know if we would ever get through. It seemed the hits just kept coming with no relief.

"Emily, you're the strongest person I know," my sister-in-law told me. I didn't feel very strong. In fact, I knew I was strong, but I was tired of being strong. Storms seemed to hit our family of 4 one right after another. I was tired and weary. I can remember crying to the Lord, "Please make it stop! Mercy, Lord!" But there wasn't any relief. The hits just kept coming.

One particularly hard season was one my husband and I faced financially. He had taken a new position in his career. In this new position the money was tight. We had always been able to go and do freely, but we were strapped. There were times when we were just praying that we would have money to be able to feed our family and make our monthly bills. It was a very tough season. We firmly held onto our faith and knew the Lord would see us through, but we were growing weary. I hate the saying, "God gives you only what you can handle" because I don't believe that. How can God show His Sovereignty if everything is easy in life? He shows His mercy and glory through our weaknesses and faith.

I remember one night sitting with my husband. We were discussing how we were going to make payments and there was an overwhelming heaviness in the air. The tension was thick. I had to get away. I had to find a quiet place to pray. As Jason and I sat discussing the bills and "what if," someone close to us sent me a picture of his wife's ultrasound. They were expecting! I shrieked with joy because they had struggled to conceive. In that very moment I heard a voice say, "Pregnant with promise."

The voice stopped me in my tracks. "Pregnant with promise? What are you saying, Lord?" I had to run. I had to find out!

When I found my quiet spot and knelt, I started praying. The Holy Spirit immediately dropped the verse:

> "'For I know the plans I have for you,' declares the Lord, 'plans to prosper you and not to harm you, plans to give you hope and a future.'"
> — Jeremiah 29:11

I was elated! A promise that I could hold onto. I didn't know what was happening, but I knew I could trust and believe that the Lord would provide a way. Sometimes the night seems long and dark but remember the promises. There is a promise in God's Word for every situation and challenge you face in life. He has made a way. He's promised you a future. He will use *all* things for His good for those that love Him (Romans 8:28) for His glory. The question remains: will you trust Him to lead the way and allow Him to use your pain?

God has a plan. Trust Him and allow Him to work.

> Dear Lord, times are hard. It's hard to see the light. Help me to see the light and let go of what I can't control. You are the Alpha and the Omega, the beginning and the end. You know my beginning and my end. You have a perfect plan for my life. Help me to trust that plan. Help me to release control and know that all things work together for my good. Thank you for providing a way and giving me wisdom to know the way.

Up
Again

-NCR

UP AGAIN

NCR

"We lose our way
   We get back up again
   It's never too late to get back up again"
   -Toby Mac

Sometimes we lose our way. Sometimes we fall down. Have you lost your way and fallen down? I want to let you know it is never too late to get back up again.

God built us all with a little resilience.

The question is, will we use it?

When we fall down will we allow the world to keep us down?

Or will we get back up again?

You can get up again.

What are some things that are keeping you down? Is it fear? Are you afraid to get back up? Are you ashamed of the fact that you have fallen? Does the difficulty of getting back up look like too much? I want to share with you some tips to help you be resilient, some tips to help you rise when the world knocks you down.

Listen up. But don't just listen to anything. John 8:32 says, "And ye shall know the truth, and the truth shall make you free." The truth and only the truth of God can set you free from the lies keeping you down. Because Satan is always trying to bombard us with lies. We need to be always surrounding ourselves with the truth. The best place to find that is in His Word. Try to spend some time in the Bible today.

Think up. Thinking negative thoughts will only make the negative time that you are going through seem worse. So, what can you do? Philippians 4:8 gives a whole list of things you can and should think about. It's more than just thinking positive thoughts. It's about thinking on things that are true, honorable, pure, and lovely, and letting those thoughts transform you (Romans 12:2).

Pray it up. If you haven't heard the song "Pray It Up" by Joel Vaughn, I encourage you to look it up and listen to it now. Prayer is just a fancy word for talking with God. And there is something about just talking with someone else and sharing your problems with someone else that makes them seem smaller. I encourage you to talk to God.

Don't give up on God. Times may be difficult. But God is always good. If you give up on God and look to something else or someone else to help you rise, let me just say, you will be disappointed. God is the only one who will never let you down. He will never disappoint you. People are not perfect. They will let you down. But God is perfect, He will never let you down. Don't give up on God.

> Lord God, I cry out to you, so many things are trying to keep me down. Lies and negative thoughts put them far away from me. Fill me, Lord, with your truth and with your thoughts, and help me to rise up again. Amen.

Rise

Up

-NCR

RISE UP

NCR

"Come on and rise up
  Take a breath, you're alive now
  Can't you hear the voice of Jesus calling us
  Out from the grave like Lazarus"
Cain

---

*L*ife is difficult. I am the oldest of nine children. In 2017 we lost our brother Clayton in a quad accident. Even though it is going on 4 years since that day, the memory of it is still fresh. Our lives and our world were never the same after that day. But that was not our only loss. We lost our Grandpa in 2018. And our uncle died in a vehicle crash right at the end of 2019.

I love a good story. Life is one big story. And in every story, there are ups and downs. A good story never ends with a low. It never ends in defeat. A good story ends on a high. It ends with a victory. Your life is a story. My life is a story. The question is, will our stories be good stories? Many things will come at us in life and try to knock us down. And we will likely get knocked down more than once in life. When life knocks you down, how do you respond? How do you react? Do you get back up again, or do you stay down? Don't let your story end in defeat.

I don't know you. I don't know your story. I don't know how many times you have been knocked down. But I do know this: Many times throughout Jesus' ministry he told people to get up and walk. My favorite example of this was when some men broke through the roof of a house that Jesus was in. They had a sick friend they wanted Jesus to heal, and the only way to get to Him was by breaking through the roof. When Jesus saw their faith He said, "Get up, take your mat, and go home." And the man got up and walked away. Both you and I do not know the future of our stories. But we do know the one who writes our stories. And we know His plans for us are good (Jeremiah 29:11 and Romans 8:28).

Stories where something bad happens to the main character and then he devotes the rest of his life trying to get his life to be normal again have always fascinated me. If there is anything that 2020 has taught me, it is that change is normal. The world around us is always changing. And we are always changing. We can't choose what will happen to us in life. And we can't change the past. But we can choose how we will respond. If life has knocked you down, I encourage you rise up. If you have fallen you need to get up again.

Lord, things have knocked me down. I know I can't change the past. I need you to help me look forward. I need you to help me rise. Amen.

Taking the First Step

-Kelly Walk Hines

TAKING THE FIRST STEP

KELLY WALK HINES

"With people it is impossible, but not with God; for all things are possible with God."
— Mark 9:23

---

*S*ix years ago, I made the most courageous, most important decision in my life.

I left. I left with only the clothes on my back and my kids. I had made a decision for my own mental health and that of my children.

It wasn't an easy choice, and it was something that needed to be done for years prior.

I had actually made the decision ten years prior to actually leaving. It literally took me that long for me to get the courage to follow through with it.

Leaving didn't magically solve all my problems but it gave me a chance to breathe and rebuild. I kept praying, kept my strength up, kept going on. I did it one day at a time.

I never gave up, no matter how dark it got, no matter how bad it hurt.

I looked back at the hard times in my life and knew that God saw me through it all. He is my strength. I am not alone.

Then one day, it just happened, the window of opportunity, and I took it.

I never looked back except to remember that I would never go back.

I used the past to remind myself of my worth and to celebrate the healing that I found.

I went from closed off and hidden to blossoming into a beautiful life.

God's love is the reason I survived all life's storms.

I always reach out my hand out for others as a beacon of hope.

No matter how dark your world is...

There is always HOPE IN THE DARKNESS!

Hope is faith in action! God gives us hope to hold onto like a life raft in rough seas.

Never give up. Never stop moving forward.

There is life after sadness, heartbreak, and loss of self!

As you heal, you will feel the strength that you have never known.

You will find happiness, like I did!

Take a quiet moment and say this prayer.

Lord, I pray that You help me see things with open eyes. Please remove obstacles that block my vision. Help me make decisions that will help me find happiness. I pray for the strength to take that first step. Carry me through this dark time.

Conquer the World

-Kelly Walk Hines

CONQUER THE WORLD

KELLY WALK HINES

"God is our refuge and strength, an ever-present help in trouble."
— Psalms 46:1-3

On a good day, I KNOW I can conquer the world.

On a bad day, I KNOW I can conquer the world, just not that day! God is always there.

I will always keep going, I will never give up! God is my strength.

God has always had my back, and I love myself enough to know that hard times will pass.

God carries me through the rough times until I am able to walk on my own.

I am more than my circumstances, more than other people's choices.

I am more than the bad things that happen to me.

No matter where I am, I will always bloom.

Remember, anything that is new and unprecedented is scary!

And guess what?

It's okay to be nervous and scared!

It's not okay to completely shut down and lose yourself.

You must keep fighting and be strong, minute by minute, hour by hour, day by day, until things make sense again.

If you are anxious, talk to someone.

If you are upset, talk with someone.

If one person won't listen, try someone else.

Keep talking until someone hears you.

Don't let anyone tell you that you are weak or wrong because you worry. That's just ridiculous, you can feel however you want.

If you are struggling, message me at hopeinthedarkness1@gmail.com. I care, I will listen.

Hard times will pass, you will be okay. We will figure out things as we go along.

The greatest gift we can give ourselves is self-love, self-acceptance, and to know our worth.

If we know that then when people exit our lives, we don't lose ourselves.

We have to make sure that our worth isn't hinged on whether someone likes us or not.

When people have an issue with you, most of the time, it's more about them than you anyway.

Regardless, things happen, people disappoint us, people hurt us, intentionally or unintentionally. When we love ourselves, we will not crumble.

This doesn't mean we won't be sad or hurt or won't have to process the grief for whatever happened. It just means you won't give up!

It just means you love yourself enough to keep fighting, you love yourself enough to know you will be okay.

Hard times come and go. We need to learn from it and grow. We must not tear ourselves down and lose our self-worth!

Resilience is fighting through the hard times and having the strength to go on.

Praying you always find hope in the darkness. 🧡

Take a quiet moment and say this prayer.

Lord, thank you for making me the way I am. I am not perfect, but I know that I am enough. Thank you, Lord, for always being there for me. I know because of you, I am worthy.

When it Rains Jump in the Puddles

-Kelly Walk Hines

WHEN IT RAINS, JUMP IN THE PUDDLES

KELLY WALK HINES

"For God gave us a spirit not of fear but of power and love and self-control."

— 2 Timothy: 1:7

One of my favorite memories of my kids growing up was when we went to storybook land. They had never been before, and we were quite excited.

The day was sunny and warm. About 30 minutes after we got there, this random set of clouds appeared, followed by rain, but no thunder.

So, I tried to get a partial refund and they said no. Everything was outside, so we had a decision to make, after it literally rained on our parade.

In these moments, you have a decision to make. You can let it ruin your day or you can embrace the change.

When I find I have these choices to make, I pray! I pray for guidance and for grace.

I remind myself God has not forsaken me and has always shown me the way.

I thought, "Well, I paid for it, so we are enjoying it." It was warm and really, the rain felt good. We didn't melt, although we were soaked. I had dry clothes in the car, but it didn't matter right at that moment.

We had a blast, caught rain on our tongues, jumped in puddles, and muddied our feet. We felt the rain and it felt welcoming after the hot sun.

Had we just run for the car at first sign of rain, I would have been out money and a lot of joy! There was so much laughter that day.

I know it's not always easy to change something bad into something good. But once you look at a situation and realize there's nothing you can do to stop the rain, it gets easier.

Just make the best of it, control what you can, make memories, and just breathe.

Take a quiet minute and pray.

Lord, I pray for a calm spirit. Please, Lord, help me to know that You have things under control. I pray that I learn to trust You in tough situations. Thank You for always being a constant in my life.

PART III
DEVOTIONAL STORIES

Be Careful What You *Ask For...*

—Mimi Emmanuel

BE CAREFUL WHAT YOU ASK FOR...

MIMI EMMANUEL

PRAYING FOR A RECHARGE AND READJUSTMENT

Getting My Back Muscles Back to Normal

Everything was going so well. After my health scares, pancreatitis, inoperable ruptured appendix, septicemia, and a variety of other ailments, I was finally recovering.

Life was once more heading in the right direction.

After nearly a decade of bed rest and being mainly home-bound, I was starting to venture out and keen to get my back muscles back to normal, and to once more participate in life fully.

All I needed was a recharge and some readjustments. I prayed for this. I hoped for this and I waited for this.

By the end of 2018, a kind friend, Dan, offered me

the chance to come along on a beach ride. Dan and my daughter go out beach riding regularly and he said, "Why don't you come along?"

"How is that even possible?" I was struggling to get around normally. On good days I could walk a little here and there, but those days were few and far between. Horse riding? Me? My back wouldn't be able to support me to sit up straight in the saddle for more than a few minutes, surely.

Dan explained to me that a few decades ago he broke his back, and that horse riding was one of the main therapies that got him back up and running again.

My daughter has been an equestrian coach for around a decade and had often mentioned that she would like to get me on a horse's back and practice equine-facilitated learning with me as well as hippotherapy. We had made some attempts, but our perfect therapy pony fell pregnant two years in a row, and that was the end of that.

Crystal had told me that riding a horse is similar to walking, without the pressure on the spine. For those of you who read *My Story of Survival, God Healed Me,* and *Live Your Best Life by Writing Your Own Eulogy,* you know that even though I got up from bed, I still had some way to go.

Our friend Dan reiterated what Crystal said, and there I went. Wow! His beautiful Percheron, Bonnie, carried me alongside the waves on the beach for way longer than I otherwise was able to sit unsupported. How was this possible?

Dan and Crystal explained to me that the movement of the horse stimulates the spine and my back. This made it possible for me to sit up unsupported, something I was not able to do without the movement of the horse's back.

It took us a few months, but finally we found two perfect horses for me to try out and hopefully with their help go on therapy rides and get my muscles back to normal.

Re-activating Nerve Endings and Muscles

If I could have picked any horse to have therapeutic rides on, it would be Coco for sure, if only she weren't so high.

I feel unsteady, and with the help of my daughter and Coco's patience, I quietly slide off her and sit on a chair in the shade, feeling excited and subdued at the same time. A minute and a half on this gorgeous animal was enough. Yes, I'm hopeful to get my back better and stimulate the nerve endings, but I haven't been on a horse for decades and this was challenging to say the least.

My daughter asks, "Have you had enough, Mum?" And to be truthful, yes, I've had enough. My gut says, "NO!" It was scarier than I thought, but I do not want to be a party pooper, so I say, "Bring it on! Lancelot's next."

"Would you rather I put a saddle on him?"

"Yes, please. It'll be less wobbly when I can put my feet in stirrups, what do you think?"

"Sure," she says. "I'll be a minute."

She saddles Lancelot up in no time at all. As soon as he is organised I am happy to get on him, being two hands shorter than Coco. I wear my brand new, charcoal-coloured jeans that I bought especially for my therapeutic horse rides.

It feels so much better sitting on a saddle with my feet in the stirrups. I feel solid but annoyed at Coco, who is breathing down my neck.

"Crystal, can you please..." Before I can finish the sentence with "tell Coco to go away..." I'm flying through the air performing an involuntary half somersault. The current of electricity surging through my back is taking my breath away. Waves of powerful charges travel up and down my spine, again and again, as I land with the back of my helmet-less head on the rocky ground.

Crystal is whispering, "This isn't happening, this isn't happening. Mum, this wasn't supposed to happen." I couldn't agree more, but the intensity and pain of the electric current that continues to surge through me makes me blurt out, "Lift me up, Crys, lift me up."

Crystal is looking at her crumpled Mum on the ground thinking, "s p i n a l i n j u r y!"

She responds, "Hell no, Mum, I'm not picking you up. You'll have to wait till we get help."

I know that if someone doesn't take the pressure of my spinal cord this unspeakable torment of currents of electricity pulsing through me from top to bottom will be the end of me. I just know.

Through gritted teeth, I spit at my daughter, "If you don't lift me up right now, you will regret this forever."

She understands and carefully places her hands underneath my armpits and ever so gently lifts my torso slowly to unfurl my spinal cord from being squashed.

This puts a stop to the electrical waves 'recharging' my system.

I start breathing again with a big sigh, "Okay, thank you, that was bad. Thank you, now don't move, don't move, don't move, STOP moving! I cannot bear it, PLEASE hold my back up." My teeth are shattering.

Crystal can't stop saying, "This wasn't supposed to happen."

And I won't, can't, let her move an inch without grinding my teeth in pain.

"I need to get help, Mum."

"You're not going anywhere. You cannot let me down. It's unbearable torture when you move. DON'T MOVE!" I hiss at her.

We're sitting on the rocky ground right at the end of the yard. Crystal is sitting on her knees, with me half reclined on her lap.

"Can you phone Stacey (my physio)?" I say, half in jest and half-serious. Surely, I'll be needing some adjustments after this tumble. My head is throbbing. My foot hurts and is tangled up in stirrups and saddle leathers etc. I'm still holding on to the saddle.

I'm wiggling my fingers and toes.

What Happened?
I Want My Six-pack Back

"Look, I can wiggle my fingers and toes. We'll be right. Praise The Lord!"

"What happened, Crys?"

"You came off, Mum."

"I know that. But how come I'm still holding the saddle?"

"'Cause the girth broke, Mum, and Lancelot bucked. I don't know what came first."

"Oh."

Sitting on my butt, I wonder, "Why does my head hurt?"

"'Cause you landed on your head, Mum."

"Oh."

I'm feeling at the back of my head for blood and find an egg-sized lump growing at the base of my skull.

"I need to phone for help, Mum."

"Yes, of course. Phone Stacey first, will you?"

"You're going to need more than a physio, Mum."

"Mpphh."

My daughter defies my orders to phone my legend of a physio.

"I need to go, Mum, and get help."

"Just phone."

"I cannot. I don't have my phone on me."

"Uh. You cannot move and leave me."

"I cannot feel my legs anymore, Mum, I need to move."

'You cannot move, not allowed to move, okay? Back says, don't move."

"Mum, I need to get help. You need to let me go."

"Hang on, let me think. Help me if you can and put the saddle underneath my back to support it just a bit... ahhh, don't move!"

I don't know how long it took to manoeuvre me to half recline on the saddle... 20 minutes, half an hour later Crystal runs to the house to phone for an ambulance.

The ambulance takes an eternity. We phone at least three times to check that they are on their way.

By the time the ambulance officers arrive, Crystal is paler than a sheet of paper. I ask if the officers can please check her out. She looks as if she's in shock. But the lovely lady ambulance officer is too busy asking me all kinds of silly questions such as the time of day, location, my name, etc.

What time is it? Time to go to the hospital.

Location? Bonanza's Ranch.

And my name? Is Miss Dumbo.

"Can I ask you a question please?"

"Sure," they say.

"I like morphine," I say. "I like it a lot. You wouldn't carry some on you, would you now?"

No worries, I'm handed a yummy green whistle with analgesic.

Bliss, it only takes a few sucks for it to work. I still feel the bruised tissue and damaged bones, but at least the edge is taken off the torment.

I'm being tied onto a stretcher and taken to the ambulance for a ride to the hospital.

I'm joking with the ambulance officer and nurses in Hervey Bay Hospital as they cut my clothes off me in the Emergency Unit. 'These weren't my favourite clothes anyway. Those brand-new jeans now know how to fall off a horse and therefore I'm happy to get rid of them.'

I don't know what they put down that drip, but it

mostly works. That is, until the nurses attempt to turn me around. We don't want bedsores, do we?

My spine does not agree, and my back lets the nurses know. Those words that come rolling out of my mouth aren't mine, they come straight from my damaged spine. Even I am shocked about that language.

This happens a few times, and after a couple of these unfortunate 'turnovers,' it is agreed by the medical team of the Spinal Unit in Brisbane that a 'stand-up' x-ray will be taken of my back. The doctor explains that I broke my back in three places and they want to make sure that the spine is okay. If the spine is stable... all good. If not, I may get a free ride in the Air Ambulance to the Brisbane Spinal Unit.

I'm not warming to this.

If I cannot tolerate nurses rolling me over, how will I appreciate a helicopter ride?

The long and the short of it is that I am not able to stand up for this 'standing-up x-ray.' Instead, I'm transferred to Maryborough Base Hospital.

ANGELS!

All I can say is that the ambulance officers and all staff at Hervey Bay and Maryborough Hospital are angels sent directly from heaven.

During my two-month stay in the hospital I'm feeling embraced, cared for, and loved by virtually everyone I come in contact with. If ever I needed a good hospital experience, this is it.

When members of the rehab unit ask me about my expectations, I tell them that I expect to leave with the sixpack I came in with. I can assure you that if I don't, it is not because of negligence from staff, but more because the sixpack I'm dreaming about hasn't been a reality of my life for quite some years.

"Mimi, what happened?"

God is good. I prayed for a re-adjustment and I certainly got one. Be careful what you pray for. Make sure that this is what you want. Be specific.

When I was catapulted off the horse on February 23, 2019, I burst vertebrae L5 and L1, and ended up with a wedged vertebra at T10. I bruised my sternum, had an egg-sized lump at the back of my head, and injured little bones in my left foot.

I'm a little shorter now. My back is still healing.

> *The entire story of my horse adventure is available for free from my website Mimi Emmanuel under https:// mimiemmanuel.com/books*

As a result of my horse fall I was gifted a beautiful recumbent trike and my puppy Mellow runs alongside me now on the foreshore of our beautiful Bay.

All's well that ends well.

My daughter and I spent years preparing for me to get involved with horse therapy. This was supposed to heal my back. Instead of healing my already delicate back, I broke it. If I can get back up and running after breaking my back in three places, anyone can!

I'm only resilient because I lean heavily on Our Father who promised me good things for my life.

"With God's help all things are possible and nothing

is impossible with God" has been my go-to-verse for the last decade and it has never let me down.

Praise Our Heavenly Father for His goodness and protection and for sending His angels to guard us.

Thank you, Father, for restoring what the locust ate and giving beauty for ashes. You are my Saviour and I thank you for helping me write the story of my life in a way that makes you proud.

Jeremiah 29:11, Luke 1:37, Matthew 19:26, Exodus 23:20, Joel 2:25, Isaiah 61:3, Psalm 91:14

You can find me on www.mimiemmanuel.com

and www.amazon.com/author/mimiemmanuel

and for freebies check out these links https://mimiemmanuel.com/books https://mimiemmanuel.com/free-tutorials

Finding Purpose in *Trauma*

-Miranda J. Chivers

FINDING PURPOSE IN TRAUMA

MIRANDA J. CHIVERS

Who comforts us in all our affliction, so that we may be able to comfort those who are in any affliction, with the comfort with which we ourselves are comforted by God. — 2 Corinthians 1:4

---

*I*n an instant, my life changed forever.

Our house was one of four across the street from the high school. My new middle school sat right behind it. The proximity allowed me to run home for lunch or engage in after-class activities. However, without the help of crosswalks or traffic warning signs, I relied on my wit and poor eyesight to dodge the zooming cars.

With the air force base only a few miles away, the rush hour was usually hectic. On the weekends, Dad's black Ford sedan—parked on the driveway alongside the road—acted as a warning; but during the week, only the big yellow buses announced the unmarked zone.

After a year of hiking through the high school yard, I'd developed a routine of greeting my new senior friends and visiting for a few minutes before heading home. Although my stomach knotted each time I crossed the road, I was confident in my predictions of when things would get busy, and the vehicular responses to my jaywalking. I had the timing down to an art.

On that sunny October afternoon, after saying good-bye to my friends, I headed to my usual point of crossing at the top of the school's driveway. At 3:30, I anticipated heavy traffic.

I positioned myself on the narrow shoulder, impatient for an opening between the long line of yellow buses as they exited the school and entered the roadway. I checked my watch again. If my timing was correct, I had exactly five minutes before the steady stream from the air base began. If I didn't cross now, I'd end up standing here forever. When another bus pulled out in front of me, and I saw the next one ready to pull out behind me, I made a run for it—even though I couldn't see the oncoming lane.

In an instant, my life changed. Tires squealed and horns blared. I froze mid-stride. My breath caught in my throat and my hands flew up into a stop signal. I turned to face the oncoming blue sedan. Four horrified faces stared back at me from behind the windshield.

I felt the scene shift into slow motion. As the car barreled into me, I instinctively jumped. The bumper connected with my legs. I flipped onto the hood, sailed across it, smacked into the windshield, then somersaulted through the air and over the roadway. I landed with a thud in the muddy ditch in front of our house. My world went dark. My heart stopped, then started again. I woke to the sound of an ambulance siren and my mother's voice praying and telling me to breathe.

In those few moments, as my spirit hovered between life and death, I glimpsed eternity as God met me with the most amazing peace and awareness of his presence. I knew the angels had helped me jump and they guided my body many meters away to the ditch—to protect me from landing underneath the car on the asphalt. I heard God say it wasn't my time to die. For the rest of my life, I would ponder the details of this surreal experience.

My survival was a miracle, but my moderate injuries were more so. Although I suffered head trauma, badly torn muscles, and extensive bruising, I had no obvious broken bones.

The following weeks blurred by as I confronted the challenges of recovery. Physical therapy was not available in our town, so I depended on my mother's practical nurse's training for direction. She encouraged me to rest for a few days before pushing me to walk and manage my own self-care.

Pain and swelling controlled my recovery. My uncoordinated body refused to take directions from my confused brain. A bumpy and painful map of black and blue gave direction to my physical healing journey. As the bruises changed color and morphed into fluid-filled lumps, they restricted my movement and complicated my use of crutches. My legs swelled so much they looked like they belonged on a purple Pillsbury dough boy.

The hidden wounds were more significant. I was afraid to fall asleep because of violent nightmares. I'd jolt awake with blood-curdling screams. My heart raced in unpredictable surges from the flood of adrenaline. During the first two weeks, Mom slept beside me to calm me during the night terrors. Constant migraines added to my agony. The doctor only prescribed mild pain medication as I was too young for anything more potent. Friends and family prayed.

Besides the excruciating muscle soreness, the psychological impact combined with the head trauma caused memory problems, confusion, irrational behavior, and poor decision-making. The unrelenting headaches and chronic fatigue left me irritable and temperamental.

My classmates dropped off my daily homework, but I couldn't focus or understand the assignments. The slow cognitive recovery compromised my return to school. Unable to concentrate or take part in physical or social activities, I felt isolated, unwanted and unimportant, like a virtual bystander to my own life. I missed my normal teenage routine. I fell into a dark depression. At fourteen and in grade nine, my life was just beginning, but I thought it was over.

On my return to class, everyone rallied to help. The teachers put a pillow on a chair so I could stretch out and elevate my legs. My classmates generously took notes and carried my books to the car. But I needed a different type of assistance that didn't exist in my academic locale.

At that time, few understood the emotional impact and the learning difficulties associated with head injuries. There were no psychologists or teachers to help me. I was like a fish out of water—fighting for air in an unfamiliar environment. I struggled to cope and study. Whereas I was once a top student, now for the first time in my academic life, I barely passed my grade.

In the days before counseling was popular, doctors treated the body expecting the mind to follow. There was no prescription for the mental agony of trauma, nor a good understanding of a damaged intellect. At my young age, I didn't have the vocabulary to explain depression and often wasn't even aware of my confused thoughts, behavior, or emotional upheaval. My worried parents watched and prayed.

As my body healed, I adapted to a new normal, discovering my own coping methods and compensatory learning strategies. Decades later, new psychological treatments would discover neuroplasticity, but at the time doctors believed that a traumatic brain injury would never recover.

The resilience of the human body is amazing. We are wired to live. I believe there is a God-implanted mechanism inside our core that encourages our bodies to heal and our minds to overcome barriers. When we tap into this power, we can climb many mountains.

The following year, my parents moved to a rural area north of town, but my accident drew attention to the city's lack of safety precautions around the busy zone. I heard the police cited the driver for a traffic violation, but my parents' conservative faith prevented them from seeking civil justice. They encouraged me to pray for the driver and his passengers and forgive them.

Part of forgiveness is understanding the part we play in our problems. When we learn to look beyond ourselves, we can see a bigger picture. I had a hard time accepting that my actions were partly responsible for my accident, but in time I could understand this and forgive myself as well.

Because trauma causes physical and emotional disruption, it's normal to experience a type of grief during recovery, including depression. I've often questioned why God allowed me to live that day. After experiencing those few moments of exhilarating serenity in his presence, I desperately wanted to die, even though I knew it wasn't my time. In other dark periods, I've been reminded that God's purpose for me is to keep going until He decides otherwise. Holding onto this tenet gives me the strength and courage to carry on.

Twenty years later, I suffered another serious crash. Once again, God intervened. Coincidently, at the time I was working as a social worker with motor vehicle accident victims. My injuries and experience gave me the compassion and insight to encourage my clients toward healing and to enable them to move beyond their tragic circumstances. God works in mysterious ways.

Fifty years after that first accident, I revisit the scene. My old house is still there. Next door on the formerly vacant property and sitting in a direct line of sight to the location of my accident, is a church. This is incredible to me. I see it as a brilliant reminder of God's intervention on that fateful afternoon.

Today, there are two crosswalks, one at each end of the high school's driveway. Across the street, on a previously empty lot, sits a gas station and convenience store. Speed limit signs with school zone flags warn drivers to slow down. Wide shoulders extend along both sides of the road, replacing the former ditch. Looking a mile down the straight route, I see the markers to the former air base and an exit to the city's bypass, which now diverts the traffic away from the school area. Today, the safety of children is paramount. I'm sad that I was the first injury to bring political attention to that dangerous area, but I'm glad that it's corrected and no longer a concern.

The book of Job shows that it's human nature to want to know the reason for tragedy and desire to blame someone or something. While trying to protect our fragile egos from the pain of admitting our sin, we project guilt and shame onto others. This paints our souls with regret and anger, and we carry these burdens into our outlook.

When we judge ourselves, we hold ourselves back and miss out on God's great promise for our future. He wants us to be intertwined with His safe design. If we trust Him to direct us where and when to cross the road, we won't get into trouble.

Some say that God allows adversity to teach us an important truth. Others say the lesson is to experience God's divine presence and know beyond any doubt that we are never alone. In my case, I learned that trusting

Him gives me the perseverance and resilience to get through anything. I literally owe Him my life.

Trauma has shifted and defined my direction; and influenced my viewpoints, my personality, and my learning style. In accepting that God has a reason for every season, I've learned to forgive the pain of the past and discover promise in the purpose. Like the roots of a tree traveling meters underground to find the nourishing spring, hardship has encouraged me to dig deep to find my spiritual strength and hold on to the one who gives me hope.

What are you holding onto?

What do you trust more: your own judgement or God's divine plan?

Pour Out Your *Heart*

-Jodi Arndt

POUR OUT YOUR HEART

JODI ARNDT

A few weeks before the holidays, I had a meltdown. I crumbled and collapsed under the weight of everything, the load too unbearable. It wasn't one particular thing, more so the piling up of small things or the lack of control over big things. Little things like clutter, laundry, and decisions over meals. Huge things like kids' education, paying medical bills, and feeling like life would never go back to "normal" after the pandemic.

I felt lost. Lost under the dirty dishes and picking up toys. Spinning and frantically angry at nothing - nothing that matters, anyway.

Overcome by emotions, I was unable to see clearly. Like towering ocean waves crashing on top of me, my eyes and throat were burning, my heart searing with pain. I felt like I was drowning, the weight of my perceived responsibility for everyone and everything crushing me. It felt like too much. Overstimulated and exhausted, I came to the edge. One last push by stress had sent me over.

A little like George Bailey ("It's A Wonderful Life") weeping as he stood on the bridge, I sat crumpled on the floor in my bedroom, sobs shaking my heart. Now, I wasn't ready to jump or give up my life like George, but I certainly felt like nothing was going right in that moment. My mind knew the truth, but stress tried to convince me otherwise. I felt as though I was wrapped in a dark shadow. I knew light was there around the corner, but at the moment it felt out of reach.

You know those days when the sun is hidden behind gray ominous clouds? You can't see it, but you know it is there, yet you still feel disheartened. On those shadowy days, darkness covers and heat lacks, making every experience feel gray, brutal, and cold. Or those bright sunny days, when suddenly everything is darker? A huge cloud has passed between you and the sun. When it is dark, clarity is elusive. You cannot see things as they truly are. Situations are not as they seem when darkness conceals and obscures. Shadow is a veil that hangs before the eyes, masking truth and parading deception as fact. On these days, like the day I was having, you have to trust that the sun is there, even when you can't see it.

It's okay to long for the sun on dark winter days. Pretending it's sunny when it's gloomy and frigid doesn't change anything. I speak the things I know, the things of which I am sure: God is Sovereign, God loves me, and God never changes. I then remind myself, "Spring will come again."

It is from these depths, the dark and sorrowful

places, that we can experience the love of Jesus the most. In the shadows of sadness or stress or being overwhelmed, the Light of Jesus shines brightest. His eyes are on us, but if we are only looking at rock bottom, we miss the rescue.

Light overcomes the darkness. When flooded with light from every direction, shadow must run.

"The light shines in the darkness, and the darkness can never extinguish it." John 1:5 NLT

So, in my moment of breaking, I opened my hands and cried out to Jesus. Knowing I could do nothing on my own, I said, "Here. I can't."

Jesus felt my anguish. When I was grieved and heartbroken, God was there with me, feeling with me. Surely if the God of all things, the Creator, my Savior and King, is crying with me, He will also show me how to get back up again. Yes, God's heart breaks. It is not a weakness, because He is perfect. Jesus allowed Himself to be human: to live, suffer, and die many years ago. Not only did He do that for us then, but He also chooses to come alongside us today in every way we live, suffer, and die as well. It is not a weakness for Him to care for us and love us. It only proves how merciful and good and faithful He is. If He didn't hold us as precious and valuable, why would He do that? It proves how much we are worth to Him.

It is okay for my heart to break. He is my ark when the waters rise around me. He scoops me up and surrounds me, through my husband's arms or encouraging words from my dear friends or sweet kisses from my sons. He pulls me from the deep waters and rescues me from the heavy burdens I have strapped to myself. He places His Word in my hands, just the right passage at just the right time. He provides, always.

> "Let all that I am wait quietly before God,
>   for my hope is in him.
>   He alone is my rock and my salvation,
>   my fortress where I will not be shaken.
>   My victory and honor come from God alone.
>   He is my refuge,
>   a rock where no enemy can reach me.
>   O my people, trust in him at all times.
>   Pour out your heart to him,
>   for God is our refuge."
> — Psalm 62:5-8 NLT

Pour out your heart to Him. He can take it.
Pour out your heart to Him. He understands.
Pour out your heart to Him. He sees you.

That day on the floor of my bedroom, I poured out my heart to Him. After I cried, I breathed. And after I breathed, I stood. And after I stood, I took a couple steps. And when I jumped back into my life after pressing pause for several minutes, the circumstances were the same. Nothing magical happened. The same things that upset me were still there. I was not spontaneously happy. I still had a million things on my to-do list. But I knew that the Lord was with me and that He knew my pain. I knew that circumstances change and these things that weighed on my heart would not stay there forever. The clouds would pass, Spring would come again.

So, after I poured out my heart to Him, I gave Him everything in trust. This was not the first time I have offered my broken fragments to Him. I know I will come to the point where I am reminded once again to do the same. But hopefully, I open my hands a little sooner each time, eventually keeping them open instead of grasping for my own control.

In desperate times, in the times you feel you can't take one more thing, let your heart break. Hold out your hands and let your heart crumble to pieces right there on your knees. It may never be the same again, but God does not want you to stay the same. He wants you to grow and trust Him more. Hand Jesus the shattered shreds and say, "Here. I can't."

He will gather the fractured splinters of your heart and restore you. He will put you back together, stronger. And because the One who created your heart is putting it back together, it will be better than before. It will break again because this world is not perfect. But Jesus is always there to catch the pieces.

When I think about bouncing back, I can't help but think of my middle son. By 6 years old he had the scars of a stuntman. His right elbow has been scabbed over so many times we lost count. Knees on concrete, nose on carpet, finger in a car door - this poor boy has been hurt repeatedly. He plays hard. He lives fully. And when you live that way, you can end up hurt frequently. For as many times as he's been hurt, you would think he'd be afraid to take risks. Not this boy. He barrels ahead, bounces back up, jumps back on. Bruises and all, he keeps going. He's the first to try something new like riding a bike or a skateboard. He can be pretty stubborn at times, but if cast in the right light, isn't stubbornness just determination? Being determined means unwilling to give up.

The bottom line? We will fall apart. We will most definitely have more thrust upon us than we can bear. Life will knock us down. How long will you stay there? Will you let fear, sadness, pressure keep you from living the life God has for you?

I want to be determined like my son: set on getting back up and trying again. I want to be honest about my own frailty and give Jesus all the control. I long for Jesus to make me like Him. I long for whatever He wants for me because I know that is what's best. I want Him to seek out the dark and selfish places still lying buried within my soul and flood them with Light. I don't want to be angry anymore. I want to be a safe place for my husband and my children. I want my hands to be free to care for others instead of gripped tightly on whatever I think I am controlling.

What is it that you are frantically trying to control? Has your heart been broken? Are you lying in the shadows in need of His Light? Ask the Lord to pick up the pieces and restore you. Pour out your heart to Him and see what He will do!

Lord, I cannot do this on my own. I have believed the deception that I have things under control. Forgive me for trusting in myself. I can do nothing apart from You. I know You see my tears. Hear my cry, God. I know Your Heart breaks with mine. Pick up the pieces of my broken heart and grant me Your peace. When I am discouraged and feel lost, may I find my strength in You because You have overcome the world. In the mighty name of Jesus, Amen.

The Power of Gratitude

-Grace Terry

THE POWER OF GRATITUDE

GRACE TERRY

*Thank God for dirty dishes. They have a tale
   to tell.
While other folks go hungry, we're eating very
   well.
With home, health, and happiness we shouldn't
   want to fuss,
For by this stack of evidence, God's very good
   to us.*

A small decorative plaque with these words hung over the stove in my mother's kitchen throughout my childhood and adolescence. When she died, it was one of the few material treasures I inherited. I probably could not have traded it for more than fifty cents, but I would not have sold it for a million dollars. It reflected my mother's philosophy and personality perfectly. I have retained the priceless lesson in its words until this very day.

My mother faced many obstacles, heartbreaks, and

hardships in life, but no matter what might test her, she always looked for and found blessings for which she gave thanks. Gratitude, faith, and scripture brought her through. Besides the little plaque, my mother gave me a living example of the power of gratitude. She modeled for me a great principle for resilience.

Both Old and New Testament scripture teaches us to give thanks. The following is just a sample of the scriptures that teach us this principle (italics added for emphasis).

"Make a joyful noise to the Lord, all you lands! *Enter into God's gates with thanksgiving and a thank offering* and into God's courts with praise! *Be thankful and say so to God,* bless and affectionately praise God's name." Psalms 100: 1, 4 (Amplified Bible)

"Speak out to one another in psalms and hymns and spiritual songs, offering praise with voices (and instruments) and making melody with all your heart to the Lord. *At all times and for everything giving thanks* in the name of our Lord Jesus Christ to God the Creator." Ephesians 5:19-20 (Amplified Bible)

> "Rejoice evermore. Pray without ceasing. *In everything give thanks*: for this is the will of God in Christ Jesus concerning you." I Thessalonians 5:16 – 18 (King James Version)

Recent rigorous scientific research has documented the power of gratitude. I'm always tickled when modern science "discovers" ancient spiritual wisdom. See, for example, this excellent article titled *"16 Benefits Of Gratitude, According To Science & Mental Health Experts."*

In spite of the good example set by my mother as well as other advantages I enjoyed growing up, I struggled with depression and anxiety beginning in early adolescence. Fortunately, I started receiving help for these and other mental health challenges in my early twenties. Over the next forty years I learned transformational life skills from spiritual teachers, mental health therapists, good books, good music, self-help groups, and physicians who prescribed appropriate medication. Without assistance from all these sources, I honestly doubt I would be alive today.

I believe God sent these healers so that I could live peacefully, joyfully, and productively, helping others on the pathway. I'm grateful that God has been very patient with me and has given me countless "second chances." When it comes to life lessons, I can be a slow learner and a quick forgetter.

One of the most important life lessons I've learned is the power of gratitude. In addition to my mother, I've been blessed with other excellent teachers.

I will always remember a time over thirty years ago when I was a newcomer at a meeting of a self-help fellowship. When I had an opportunity to talk, I immediately launched into a lengthy description of my challenges with depression. The group listened kindly and patiently. Eventually, I finished my monologue and passed so that someone else could talk.

When the meeting ended, an "old-timer" in the group walked up to me and smilingly asked, "Do you know what depression is?" By this time in my life I was a licensed mental health professional, so I thought I did know a few things about depression. However, she had caught me off guard so I responded with something brilliant like, "Huh?"

She said, "Depression is terminal self-pity. The cure is gratitude." Still smiling, she drifted away. I felt as if I had been banged in the face by a frying pan. Driving home from the meeting, I seethed with indignation. *How dare she...??*

When I calmed down enough to reflect, I had to admit to myself she was right – I did frequently indulge in toxic self-pity. In fact, you might say that I had elevated self-pity to a fine art!

My next thought was, if she was right about that maybe she's also right about the cure being gratitude. Maybe I will try that. So I started a daily practice of counting my blessings, looking for things for which to give thanks.

The results were immediate and dramatic. My depression became much easier to manage. Today, looking back, I am extremely grateful for that smiling lady who nailed me. I believe she was sent by God. I'm glad I paid attention.

This is not to discount or minimize the seriousness of clinical depression. As stated before, I have received on-going assistance from many sources (all sent by God) to help me learn to manage my depression, anxiety and other health challenges. This is simply to say that learning to practice gratitude, which is simple and doable for anyone, has been and continues to be one of the most powerful tools in my toolbox.

To add this practice to your toolbox, I recommend keeping a gratitude journal for a minimum of thirty days. Get a notebook or tablet or calendar and for thirty days write down five or more NEW things for which you are grateful. Each item can be placed on the thirty-day list only once. It doesn't have to be anything huge. It can be little things that you normally neglect to notice. You will find yourself giving thanks for things you previously have taken for granted. You will brighten your own day and will also be a light shining from the inside out for others.

Another time I attended a self-help meeting a young woman shared this, "I'm so grateful that I was able to take a shower today. Not long ago I was living on the street and I had no way to take a shower. Today I sometimes take two showers a day and I'm thankful...." Again, this was over thirty years ago but to this day I carry that young woman's message in my heart. I often remember her and thank God that I can take a nice, warm shower whenever I like.

To get you started in your gratitude journal, here are some suggestions.

1. Thank God for life, for the opportunity to breathe, learn, laugh, love, and participate in this adventure.
2. Be thankful for your body and its infinite miracles - your senses, cells, organs, and organ systems which synchronize so that your spirit has an earthly home for a time. Even if you have physical health challenges, your life force is greater than your death force or you would not be alive. Be grateful for everything in your body that is working for you. Focus on your health instead of your health challenges. When you really start thinking about all the things about your physicality for which to be grateful, you could get several days' lists on this one topic alone.
3. Be grateful to God for your character strengths, your perseverance, your unique beauty, your sense of humor, your creativity and any and all other assets. You have these assets to some degree or you would not have survived this long.
4. I'm assuming you can read. Be thankful to God for your ability to read and understand what you read. Be grateful for books, periodicals, libraries and librarians.
5. Thank God for the beauty of nature. Look around you with an open heart and mind and you can use the natural world to make your list for several days.
6. Thank God for inspiring artists, musicians,

poets, writers, filmmakers, actors, and other creatives who enrich your life.

7. Appreciate and give thanks to God for *every single person* who has ever made a positive difference in your life. Verbally express your appreciation to them and/or send thank you notes, cards, or letters. So many people are starving for acknowledgment and appreciation. You cannot know what your expressions of gratitude can mean to those who have made a difference for you, but certainly you will know how rewarding it is to say or write those words from your heart.

8. Be grateful to God for every person or situation that has ever tested or a tried or challenged you. If you survived the test or the trial, you learned or re-learned a valuable lesson. Be thankful for the lessons and pray for those who tested or tried you.

If you will make your list of five or more new things for which you are grateful for at least thirty days, you will have developed an "attitude of gratitude" that will serve you well all your days. You will also be much better equipped to make a positive difference in the lives of others.

On a recent cold gray day I wanted nothing so much as to stay home, snug and warm and dry with my sweetheart and four-legged angels. However, I had already procrastinated for several days about going to the grocery store, so I suited up and headed out. On the way to the store it started sprinkling rain. *Great!*

I had a long list of items to find and the store was out of stock for several of them. I spent what seemed like a lot of time trudging up and down the aisles to be sure I wasn't overlooking the items I sought. As I rounded an aisle at the front of the store I could see out the front windows that it was now raining harder. *Oh, wonderful!*

Trudging up and down the aisles, I heard myself think the thought, *"I HATE buying groceries. ..."* WHOA! Time for an attitude adjustment. I immediately went into my attitude of gratitude mode.

My next thoughts were, "I'm so grateful that I can buy groceries. I have a reliable car that brought me to the grocery store. I have gasoline in my car. I have the money to buy groceries. I have the physical health and stamina to buy groceries. I have the mental health to function in the world. Even though a few things on the list are out of stock, I'm able to find the huge majority of the grocery items on my list. Many of the items are being offered at a special price today. The store is not crowded and every person with whom I've interacted has been pleasant and courteous. I remembered to wear my water repellant jacket. I'm so fortunate to be here buying groceries ..."

By the time I reached the checkout, I was smiling and could respond courteously and with sincere appreciation to the cashier and the young lady who sacked my groceries. Having consciously cultivated the practice of gratitude for many years, this tool stays sharp and is always ready when needed.

If you have any doubt as to how powerful your gratitude can be for the entire human family, I have one more story from my personal experience to share. Many years ago I was working as a social worker at a community agency. Occasionally my duties took me to a community health clinic which served low income families.

One morning, I approached the clinic walking up the sidewalk toward the front door. Just as I opened the door from the outside, a short, round, middle-aged, black lady arrived at the door from inside the clinic. I automatically stepped aside, held the door open for her to exit the building, and said, "Good morning, how are you?" She beamed at me and in a sweet voice exuding gratitude and good cheer, she replied, "I'm *BLESSED*, baaybee!" as she stepped out the door and floated by.

Operating on autopilot, I stepped inside the clinic and let the door close behind me. I stood still just inside that door for several moments. I was absolutely stunned by the positive energy radiating from that woman's being. I have no way of knowing, but I believe that dear soul must have been practicing gratitude for many years in order to have the spiritual power she projected that day.

I could feel the energy of her genuine gratitude vibrating in every cell of my body! I have not been the same person since. In a moment, I was changed forever. It took several years for me to begin to integrate the impact of that brief encounter into my heart and mind and spirit. I'm still in the process of integrating it.

I have told this story on many occasions in many different settings and I included it in my recently published book *"Ten Simple Strategies for a Happier You."* If even one person in an audience or one reader really gets it, then it is worth telling. Every time I tell the story, I internalize the lesson again, at deeper and higher levels.

...and now when someone asks me how I am doing, more often than not, I smile and say enthusiastically "I'm *BLESSED*, Baaybee!" (I'm now at a wonderful age when I can call just about anyone "baby" without offense.) My prayer is that at least once in my lifetime, I might have the impact on someone else that the beautiful short, round, middle-aged, African-American angel had on mine.

Are you willing to transform your own life and have a life-changing impact on other individual lives as well as a redemptive influence on the entire human family? If so, practicing gratitude is one powerful tool for your tool chest.

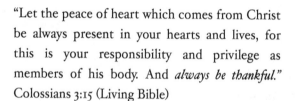

"Let the peace of heart which comes from Christ be always present in your hearts and lives, for this is your responsibility and privilege as members of his body. And *always be thankful.*" Colossians 3:15 (Living Bible)

Curve Balls

-Leisa Williams

CURVE BALLS

LEISA WILLIAMS

Many curve balls may be thrown at us in life. How we respond to such circumstances reveals much about our inner coping mechanisms and shows others who we indeed are when we come under pressure. For example, if you squeeze an orange, what comes out? Orange juice, of course, not lemon or apple juice because what comes out is what is inside the fruit, orange juice! The inside really matters because if lemon juice were to come out of oranges, what is expected to be sweet and delicious is tart and sour. The outer is not reflecting what is really on the inside.

We may look like we have it all together on the outside, but when the storms of life hit, how resilient are you?

When life puts the 'squeeze' on us, it can be humbling to see what comes out under such pressure. Is it anger, bitterness, fear?

Ask yourself, "Do I come under the circumstances

rather than growing more resilient through the events? Where do I find my strength? When faced with adversity in life, how do I cope or adapt?

Why do I think that some people seem to bounce back from tragic events or loss much more quickly than others? Why may it seem that some people seem to get "stuck" at a point in their life without the ability to move forward?"

Learning to place my hope and trust in Christ has been key to me developing resilience to handle whatever circumstances come across my path, especially as I meditate on the words of Jesus.

> "I have said these things to you, that in Me you may have peace. In the world you will have trouble. But take heart; I have overcome the world."
> —John 16:33 ESV

And consider the fact that no matter what 'troubles' Jesus had (and He had many), he did not sin.

> "For we do not have a high priest who cannot sympathize with our weaknesses, but One who has been tempted in all things as we are, yet without sin."
> — Hebrews 4:15

Jesus was a very resilient person!

As I share a little of my story from this past year, I pray that it may encourage you to turn your eyes upon Jesus amid your circumstances. May you be encouraged to persevere in troubled times and learn to allow the one who made us and loves you to bear His image through your circumstances. This is so that we can become people who, when under pressure, live lives that resemble the one who knew the most about being resilient, Jesus! As His image bearers we can shine His light and give hope to others in their difficulties.

The summer of 2020 was filled with smoke and haze and the ever-present threat of fire. Canberra, Australia was declared a state of emergency in the Australian bush capitol, as massive bushfires threatened to become uncontrollable amid high temperatures and strong winds. Residents lived for many weeks with their cars packed ready for an emergency evacuation as houses and properties burned in surrounding areas. The thick smoke was oppressive, and fear and anxiety crept upon us once more. We were all so relieved when summer finally drew to a close, as the horror bushfire season claimed houses and lives and took its toll mentally and emotionally on us all.

It was 3 a.m. on the 9th of March 2020, and I remember stirring in my sleep and feeling a distinct sense of overwhelm. Then a strange calm came upon me, and the Holy Spirit reassured me, it would be okay, I would come through what was to come. Little did I know that my father was struggling for his final breaths. His battle with leukemia was about to end and he would within hours slip into the arms of his Heavenly Father.

I live some four days' drive (or five hours in a plane) away from where my parents lived. That morning I had breakfast and went to work. Later that morning, I received a text to say that Dad was not well and was being taken to hospital. It was fully expected that he would be home in a couple of days. By lunch we were told he would not make it and come quickly. I dropped everything and booked a flight. He had gone before my taxi had arrived to take me to the airport.

I thank you, God, for answering my prayers for Dad that he would go quickly. I was thankful to God for the assurance He is loved, accepted, and forgiven. It was God ordained that Mum and Dad's pastor was present to support her and pray with Dad as he left this earth.

I released Dad into His loving care and asked that in His time He would lift the grief and loss from those of us who loved him and fill our hearts with joy and peace as we so fondly remember Dad. Thanking Jesus that because of His selfless sacrifice on the cross where He took our sin and conquered death, Dad is now seated with Him in the heavenly places.

This all happened one week before my son and now daughter-in-law was to be married—a big Italian wedding with many guests. Instead, we found ourselves near the top end of Australia with all my extended family at a funeral and a wake, mourning, celebrating the life of Dad. To lighten the moment there were quips made about it being like 3 weddings and a funeral, only the funeral came first.

Little did we know flying home that we were on one of the very last flights into Canberra. The coronavirus had been declared a pandemic, and there were rumours of the travel industry locking down. The flight was eerily quiet, and the air stewards were uncertain as to whether they would have a job, for many it would be their last flight. Business-class food was shared amongst the passengers in the economy to run down the supplies, it was bewildering and hard to grasp what was to come.

One week later, three days before our son's wedding, our country went into lockdown. Months of planning for a much-anticipated celebration faded before our eyes. The Prime Minister announced that within 24 hours no more than five people would be allowed to attend a wedding, including the bridegroom and photographer. My son called, "Can you make it to Sydney tomorrow? We are getting married." Hours before the lockdown, ten of us gathered in a relative's backyard for the wedding, including aging grandparents who may not see their grandchild married should it be delayed. One grandparent had already died, when for months our family had been saying, "See you at the wedding." We all thought we would see Dad one last time there.

We did not want to risk not having another grandparent be able to see their grandchildren married. A small ceremony went ahead with no celebration or food. Yet, they were married, praise the Lord!

As a teacher, I very quickly had to adjust my work to home and develop learning at home programs for my students. Some days we had Zoom meetings happening simultaneously in most rooms of our home as my husband is also a teacher. Between classes, studies, and general family life, we were being stretched every which way, especially with the grief and loss of Dad and the wedding celebrations we so had looked forward to. To top it all off, I discovered that I needed to have a hysterectomy. I ended up having a term off work to recover.

I have heard it said, "Who you are under pressure is who you are." Throughout this season, I had to daily come to God and pour out what I was really thinking and feeling. It was essential, to be honest, and real with God, so that I could process the difficulties we were going through. Life was not only just threatening to knock us down, but millions of people across the planet, some who could not bounce back from their circumstances. I had to take my eyes off myself and put them onto Jesus.

A PATHWAY TO BUILDING RESILIENCE

These tips can be a starting point to build resilience in your life:

1. ACKNOWLEDGE AND ACCEPT THE CIRCUMSTANCES –

Jesus acknowledged to the Heavenly Father how He felt and accepted His circumstances.

"My soul is overwhelmed with sorrow to the point of death" (Mt. 26:38). "My Father, if it is possible, may this cup be taken from me. Yet not as I will, but as You will" (Mt 26:39 NIV).

II. Stay Calm

Jesus was calm and managed His emotions. If Jesus says it is possible to not be anxious then it must be possible.

> "Do not be anxious about anything, but in everything by prayer and supplication with thanksgiving, let your requests be made known to God. And the peace of God, which surpasses all understanding, will guard your hearts and your minds in Christ Jesus."
> Philippians 4:6-7 (ESV)

III. Be Real

Jesus was real about his circumstances. He did not bottle them up but poured them out to His Father. That may mean expressing anger, grief, fear, etc. It is essential to be honest with yourself and God. What you really think and feel is valid. Remember God knows you...

> "But let him who boasts boast of this, that he understands and knows Me, that I am the LORD who exercises lovingkindness, justice, and righteousness on earth; for I delight in these things," declares the LORD" (Jeremiah 9:24 NIV).

IV. Trust God

Trusting Him by praising Him for what He is doing, that His ways are higher even when you cannot see a way forward. Jesus is a light in the darkness and learning to trust in Him when things are rugged builds resilience. Then Jesus again spoke to them, saying, "I am the **Light** of the world; he who follows Me will not walk in the **darkness**, but will have the **Light** of life."

When we place our trust in Jesus, no matter what our circumstances are, we will become more resilient people. The below Scripture says our roots will be strong and deep. We will not be uprooted when the curve balls come, instead we learn to place our hand in the one who made us and trust in Him to sustain us. Take a moment to reflect on this Scripture, you may even like to pray it as a prayer.

"But blessed is the man who trusts me, GOD, the woman who sticks with GOD. They are like trees replanted in Eden, putting down roots near the rivers— Never a worry through the hottest of summers, never dropping a leaf, Serene and calm through droughts, bearing fresh fruit every season."

—Jeremiah 17:7-8-7-8 The Message (MSG)

In Jesus' Name, Amen!

Throw out Your Calenders

-Leisa Williams

THROW OUT YOUR CALENDARS

LEISA WILLIAMS

Each January I sit down and enter into my calendar all the commitments, events, holidays, etc., that I have pre-planned for the year. With electronic calendars it is so much easier to pre-plan and I have some appointments scheduled into 2021 already.

Yet this year it is almost like we have had to throw our calendars in the bin as all the plans have either had to be cancelled, postponed, adjusted, or laid down. We had to lay down all expectations of what our son's wedding would be like and all the anticipation and joy of celebrating with close family and friends was laid down, a time I had really looked forward to and still was very special, but not like we thought.

As you know, many people didn't have what we were blessed with, and I know of some very sad brides who, though they know the party will come, couldn't even have their parents at the ceremony. Yet every day I am reminded to count my blessings, offer them up God. To awake each new day and tell God thank you!

As someone once said to me, at the very least, I can be thanking God for the breath in my lungs. Many in our world may be struggling for that breath, yet in Job 33:4 we read "the Spirit of God has made me, the breath of the Almighty gives life" (NIV). If you are struggling to breathe either health-wise or you feel choked by life's circumstances, can I encourage you to ask God to breathe His life into your situation?

Even in this difficult season, as I watch the plans I made for 2020 and beyond shift and change, I'm choosing/learning to trust God and take heart in these words from Scripture.

As Isaiah 55:8-9 says, "'My thoughts are not your thoughts, neither are your ways My ways,' declares the Lord. 'As the heavens are higher than the earth, so are My ways higher than your ways and My thoughts than your thoughts'" (NIV).

Jeremiah 29:11 says,

"For I know the plans I have for you, plans to prosper you and not to harm you, plans to give you a hope and a future" (NIV).

This well-quoted verse was written by Jeremiah to the Israelites while they were in exile. What this means is that God has plans for a whole group of people, namely the nation of Israel. And if we read on in the Scriptures, we find that this promise was fulfilled: those in exile returned, and the nation of Israel was restored for a time. God made a promise through the prophets, and that promise came true, after 70 years.

God is a God of redemption, after all, and He wants to redeem people and put them on a path of wholeness, just as He wanted the nation of Israel to be redeemed and whole again.

Many of us desperately want to know the plan that God has for each one of us as individuals, but let the prophet Jeremiah remind us that it's not all about us, and it might not look like what we think.

Even more important than our decision about which college to attend, which city to move to, or what job offer to take is the future hope of the Kingdom of God foretold by the prophets and fulfilled in the reign of our now and coming King. In this way, the promise of Jeremiah 29:11 is bigger than any one of us—and far better.

So in light of Jeremiah 29:11, perhaps, we can see God's hand in this season. I encourage you to look at the good or positive things that have occurred as a result of the pandemic, which enabled us to have a more balanced perspective on this season, that it may not be all bad and not just all about us.

I took some time with the Lord and symbolically threw my 2020/21 calendar in the bin. I realised that it was symbolic of laying all my hopes, dreams, fears, aspirations, etc., at His feet that I had had for 2020.

As our perspective comes in line with God's, we may begin to see our dreams fulfilled. So, act on your plans and your vision, but remain open to God's course-altering perspective—and let it guide your way.

However, remember we are all in this together. This verse does not apply to isolated individuals or to a broad community. It applies to both, together, functioning as one, the body of Christ.

This season for many of us may be a reset, a time of

bringing our plans into alignment with Gods, seeking Him for His will, perhaps in a deep place of surrender to Him to allow Him to bring forth change in this year and our lives for all that He desires, not our striving for our own agenda, but offering hope personally and corporately.

It can be scary coming to the place where our fear of whatever is surrendered to Him, that our control is being surrendered and is replaced by trust, a much deeper trust in God and His word.

But if we allow ourselves to come to this place of surrender, it leaves room for God to move and change our perspective and realise that the hope and future, from an eternal perspective, is way bigger than we can ever imagine.

From this standpoint we become resilient people, aware of our emotional reactions to life's circumstances and trusting in God no matter what the circumstances. Part of being resilient is understanding that life is full of challenges. This self-awareness is essential because it helps you to see yourself clearly and honestly. When we adopt this posture of surrender it enables God to mould and shape us into the people that He has destined us to be, despite the circumstances we may find ourselves in.

> Heavenly Father, Help me to become a more resilient person by learning to trust in You much more deeply amidst my circumstances. I understand that life is full of challenges, but You breathe Your life into them all when we come to you. In Jesus Name, Amen!

FREE DEVOTIONALS AND STORIES

Want an advance copy of the next Devo Writers Collaboration for free?!

Go to *read.ChristWriters.com*

Subscribe to get:

- advance copies of Devo Writers Collaborations
- author interviews and special offers
- invitations to participate however you'd like

JOIN THE NEXT COLLECTION

Join the next collection! Go to DevoWriters.com to see how to get involved.

Check out the Facebook Group, Devo Writers Collaborations to follow along and see how you can contribute:

facebook.com/groups/christiancollections

If you're an author and have any self-publishing needs, contact michael@michaellacey.me.

LAST REQUEST

People need to build Resilience, cultivate Hope, and grow in Faith. The more reviews, the more readers we can attract.

To do your part, please leave an honest review on Amazon!

Thank you!